SOCIAL STUDIES

Also by Fran Lebowitz

METROPOLITAN LIFE

SOCIAL STUDIES

Fran Lebowitz

SIDGWICK & JACKSON
LONDON

First published in Great Britain in 1982
by Sidgwick and Jackson Limited

Originally published in the United States of America
in 1981 by Random House

ISBN 0-283-98829-0

Printed in Great Britain by
A. Wheaton and Co. Ltd, Exeter
for Sidgwick and Jackson Limited
1 Tavistock Chambers, Bloomsbury Way
London, WC1A 2SG

In memory of Henry Robbins

CONTENTS

PLACES

IDEAS

PEOPLE

PEOPLE

*P*eople (a group that in my opinion has always attracted an undue amount of attention) have often been likened to snowflakes. This analogy is meant to suggest that each is unique—no two alike. This is quite patently not the case. People, even at the current rate of inflation—in fact, people especially at the current rate of inflation—are quite simply a dime a dozen. And, I hasten to add, their only similarity to snowflakes resides in their invariable and lamentable tendency to turn, after a few warm days, to slush.

This is, I am aware, though not a particularly popular sentiment, also not exactly a novel one either. I do believe, however, that this is the very first time it has ever been expressed with an intention to substantiate it with well-documented written evidence. In other words, everybody talks about people but nobody ever does anything about them.

What I have decided to do is to point out that except in extremely rare instances people are pretty much like everyone else. They all say the same things, have the same names and wear their hair in the same styles. This is not a modern phenomenon but one that has been true throughout all of history. This can clearly be seen in the following orderly fashion:

I. WHAT PEOPLE SAY

Below you will find the complete and unabridged record of the general conversation of the general public since time immemorial:

    a. Hi, how are you?
    b. I did not.
    c. Good. Now you know how I felt.
    d. Do you mind if I go ahead of you? I only have this one thing.

II. WHAT PEOPLE ARE CALLED

This varies from era to era but at any given time almost everyone has the same name. Your average Joe has simply become your average Jennifer. In more ways than one.

III. HOW PEOPLE WEAR THEIR HAIR

When it comes to hair, the possibilities are not, fortunately, endless. And while this may be news to sportscasters and hairdressers, it is nevertheless a fact. The evidence is overwhelmingly conclusive and this list proves it.

    People Who Have or Have Had Almost
    the Exact Same Hairstyle
    a. Victor Hugo and Sarah Caldwell
    b. William Wordsworth and Frank Lloyd Wright

c. W. B. Yeats and David Hockney
d. Jean Cocteau and Eli Wallach
e. Johan August Strindberg and Katharine Hepburn
f. Pablo Picasso and my maternal grandfather, Phillip Splaver

All of the above is true; and if you don't believe me, you can look it up for yourself.

Now that we have learned these elementary lessons, most of you are probably asking yourselves the question, "Well, then, in what ways *do* people differ from one another?" There are two answers to this question. First of all, everyone has a different—and yes, even unique—size foot. In fact, no two feet are exactly alike—not even, as you have probably discovered, your own two feet. Every single human foot has its own inimitable size, its own distinctive shape, its own little personality. *Feet* are like snowflakes. Your feet, more than anything else, are what make you you, and nobody else's are quite like them.

The second thing that distinguishes you, sets you apart from the crowd, is that everybody in the entire world likes his eggs done a different and special way. When it comes to eggs, everyone has his own subtle preference, his own individual taste. So the next time that someone asks you how you like your eggs, speak right up. After all, you only go around once.

It is at this juncture that many of you may now be thinking that the state of affairs thus far described is a sorry one indeed. Wouldn't things be a whole lot better, you may be asking, if, say, egg preferences were uniform but conversation somewhat more varied? Yes, things certainly would be a whole lot better, and yet, although there is a solution to this problem, it is one that could only be brought about by the greatest mutual effort. The solution is this: I will supply a short course in conversational uplift if you will all decide on one universal way you like your eggs. I realize, of course, that it will be difficult for such a diverse and colorful group of foot sizes to come to such an agreement, but if you promise to at least try, I too will do my best.

Before we tackle the larger and more comprehensive issues of conversation, I feel that a few words on the subject of trying too hard might well be in order.

Trying Too Hard

The conversational overachiever is someone whose grasp exceeds his reach. This is possible but not attractive.

———

Original thought is like original sin: both happened before you were born to people you could not possibly have met.

———

The Larger and More Comprehensive Issues

Great people talk about ideas, average people talk about things, and small people talk about wine.

———

Polite conversation is rarely either.

———

Spilling your guts is just exactly as charming as it sounds.

———

Never name-drop at the dinner table. The only thing worse than a fly in one's soup is a celebrity.

———

The only appropriate reply to the question "Can I be frank?" is "Yes, if I can be Barbara."

———

Telling someone he looks healthy isn't a compliment—it's a second opinion.

———

Looking genuinely attentive is like sawing a girl in half and then putting her back together. It is seldom achieved without the use of mirrors.

———

The opposite of talking isn't listening. The opposite of talking is waiting.

———

HOW NOT TO MARRY A MILLIONAIRE: A GUIDE FOR THE MISFORTUNE HUNTER

*T*he marriage of a well-known Greek shipping heiress and an unemployed Russian Communist has given rise to the speculation that we may, in fact, be witnessing an incipient trend. It is not unlikely that working your way down may shortly become the romantic vogue among the truly rich—with interest ranging from the merely less fortunate to the genuinely poor. Should this become the case, our more affluent brethren will undoubtedly be in need of some practical advice and careful guidance. Thus I offer the following course of instruction:

I. WHERE POORER PEOPLE CONGREGATE

Meeting the poorer person is a problem in itself, for the more conventional avenues of acquaintance are closed to you. The poorer person did not prep with your brother, form a racehorse syndicate with your broker or lose to you gracefully in Deauville. He does not share your aesthetic interest in pre-Columbian jewelry, your childhood passion for teasing the cook or your knowledge of land values in Gstaad. Therefore, it is not probable that the poorer person is someone whom you are just going to run into by chance. He must be actively sought. In seeking the poorer person, one must be ever mindful of both his habits and his daily routine:

a. The very backbone of the mass-transit system *is* the poorer person, who when he must go somewhere will usually avail himself of the vivid camaraderie to be found on buses and subways. Should you choose this method, take special care that you do not give yourself away by an awkward and superfluous attempt to hail the E train or by referring to the bus driver as "the captain."

b. The poorer person performs most personal services for himself. Thus he can commonly be found in the acts of purchasing food, laundering clothing, shopping for hardware, picking up prescriptions and returning empty bottles. These tasks can be accomplished at locations throughout the city and are all open to the public, which can, if you like, include yourself.

c. Generally speaking, the poorer person summers where he winters.

d. Unless he's an extremely poorer person (i.e., a welfare recipient) he will spend a substantial portion of each day or night at work. Work may occur in any number of places: stores, offices, restaurants, houses, airports or the front seats of taxicabs. With the possible exception of the last, you yourself have easy and frequent access to all such locales—a circumstance that can often be used to advantage, as it affords you the opportunity of making that crucial first gesture.

II. BREAKING THE ICE WITH POORER PEOPLE

In approaching the poorer person, one can employ, of course, the same tactics that one might use in approaching someone on more equal footing with oneself. Charm, wit, tact, direct eye contact, simple human warmth, the feigning of interest in his deeper feelings—all of these may be beneficial in establishing rapport. Such strategies are, however, not without risk, for they are every one open to misinterpretation and most certainly cannot be counted upon for immediate results. Poorer people, being, alas, not only poorer but also people, are quirky; they too have their little moods, their sore spots, their prickly defenses. Therefore their responses to any of the above might well be erratic and not quite all that one has hoped. Do not lose heart, though, for it is here that your own position as a richer person can best be exploited and can, in fact, assure you of almost instantaneous success in getting to know the poorer person more intimately.

Buy the poorer person an expensive present: a car; a house; a color television set; a dining-room table. Something nice. The poorer person, without exception, loves all these things. Buy him one of them and he will definitely like you enough to at least chat.

III. WHAT NOT TO SAY TO POORER PEOPLE

It is at this juncture that the utmost care be exercised lest you lose your hard-won toehold. For it is in actual conversation with the poorer person that even the most attentive and conscientious student tends to falter.

Having been softened up with a lavish gift, the poorer person will indeed be in an expansive, even friendly, frame of mind. He is not, however, completely and irrevocably yours yet; it is still possible to raise his hackles and make as naught all of your previous efforts. A thoughtless remark, an inopportune question, an unsuitable reference—any of these may offend the poorer person to the point where you may totally alienate him. Below are some examples of the sort of thing one really must strive to avoid:

a.   Is that your blue Daimler blocking the driveway?

b.   . . . and in the end, of course, it's always the larger stockholder who is blamed.

c.   I'll call you around noon. Will you be up?

d.   Who do you think you are, anyway—Lucius Beebe?

e.   Don't you believe it for a minute—these waiters make an absolute fortune.

f.   Oh, a uniform. What a great idea.

IV. A SHORT GLOSSARY OF WORDS USED BY POORER
   PEOPLE

sale—An event common to the retail business, during the
   course of which merchandise is reduced in price. Not to
   be confused with *sail,* which is, at any rate, a good word
   not to say to poorer people.

meatloaf—A marvelously rough kind of pâté. Sometimes
   served hot.

overworked—An overwhelming feeling of fatigue; exhaus-
   tion; weariness. Similar to jet lag.

rent—A waste of money. It's so much cheaper to buy.

THE FOUR GREEDIEST CASES: A LIMITED APPEAL

Angela de G.

I t is quiet now in the almost devastated East River co-op. Tarps litter the seriously marred parquet floors. Paint-stained ladders stand like skeletons in the somber dimness of insufficient track lighting. Abandoned shades of gray sadly spot a lower wall. Forlorn swatches of fabric in a harsh jumble of acid greens and impenetrable blacks are strewn angrily across a veritable ruin of an Empire Récamier. It is quiet now. Yes. Now. But for Angela de G., the occupant of this cavernous wreck, the momentary quiet is but an all too brief interlude. A precious chunk of serenity in a world that has turned upside down. A world made chaotic and unsure. A world of terror and bleakness. A world of despair.

Angela de G. is renovating.

Quietly the small figure sits huddled in a huge coffee-colored sweater that is much too big for her emaciated frame. A sweater so voluminous and ill-fitting that one can barely hear her speak—a sweater, alas, that she could hardly refuse no matter how wretched the cut, how unflattering the hue, how inappropriate the garment to her way of life.

It was a gift from the designer.

But Angela de G., as she stares out the window, across the freezing black river and into the bleakness of Queens, seems oblivious to her attire. So great is her present crisis, so encompassing her depression that it is almost—almost—as if even clothes didn't matter any more.

As Angela de G. talks, one is immediately struck by the conflict in her voice—low in volume but loud in agony as she pours out her litany of despair—a tale all too familiar to those of us in the social services. Familiar, yes, but nonetheless heartrending, for Angela de G.'s pain is real, her burden heavy. So one listens and one hears. Hears it all—the bitter fighting between the decorator and the architect, the arrogance of the lighting designer, the workmen who are late, the painters who are clumsy. The time and a half, the double time, the shock of hitherto unconsidered legal holidays. Yes, one listens, one hears, and one does, of course, what little one can. Hesitantly, all too aware of the meagerness of one's assistance, the terrible inadequacy of one's own ability to cope with such a situation, one offers what is, after all, cold comfort. The name of a little man marvelous with parquet. The number of a nonunion plumber in Newark. The hope that she will someday find an upholsterer who knows what he's doing. Yes, one tries. One makes an effort, puts up a good front. But one knows, finally, that it will take more. That outside aid is needed. And needed badly.

Angela de G. is renovating.

Won't you please help?

Leonard S.

Leonard S. is alone. Very alone. All alone. Yes, Leonard S. is by himself now. It was not always this way. Once it was different. Quite different. Last night, in fact. But all that has changed now. All that is over. For this morning, when Leonard S. awoke, he was confronted head-on with a tragedy he had long been dreading. Christopher R. was gone. Yes, Christopher R., dear, sweet, beautifully proportioned Christopher R. had left and Leonard S. was alone. Christopher R., however, was not alone. He was with all of Leonard S.'s cash, half of Leonard S.'s wardrobe, Leonard S.'s portable color television set, and Leonard S.'s exquisite little Ingres drawing.

Leonard S. hopes Christopher R. is happy now.

Happy with the way he's treated Leonard S. Happy with the lies, the deceptions, the cheating. Happy with the way he's hustled Leonard S.—used his connections, his credit-card number, his account at Paul Stuart's. Happy with his adolescent arrogance, happy with his unspeakable ingratitude, happy with his exquisite little Ingres drawing.

Leonard S. is not happy. He is depressed. He is sick and he is tired. He is headachey. His illusions are shattered. His trust has been violated. He doesn't feel like going to work. He is a broken man like a million other broken men in a cold, unfeeling city. He is unbearably low. He is suffused with gloom. And he just can't face the studio today.

Leonard S. talks, and his pain is a terrible thing to witness. Leonard S. loved Christopher R. Cherished him, cared for him, supported him. Leonard S. thought Christopher R. was loyal. Thought he was decent, thought he was different. Different from the others. Different from Timothy M., John H., Rodney W., David T., Alexander J., Matthew C., Benjamin P. and Joseph K. Different from Ronald B., from Anthony L. and from Carl P. But he was wrong. Very wrong.

He sees that now.

He must have been blind. He must have been crazy. He must have been out of his mind.

The phone rings.

Leonard S. returns from the call and it is apparent that tragedy has struck again. He pours himself a drink. His hands shake. His eyes are twin pools of anguish. He can barely speak, but slowly the sordid story is told. He has been doubly betrayed. What little faith he had left has deserted him completely. Christopher R. is en route to Los Angeles. With Leonard S.'s heart. With all of Leonard S.'s cash. With half of Leonard S.'s wardrobe. With Leonard S.'s portable color television set. With Leonard S.'s exquisite little Ingres drawing.

And with Leonard S.'s assistant, Michael F.

Leonard S. says he is through. He says he is finished. He says nothing means anything to him anymore—nothing at all. But perhaps there is yet some hope. Perhaps *you* can help. All contributions are in the strictest confidence. Anonymity is assured. We dare not speak your last name.

Mr. and Mrs. Alan T.

There was laughter here once. Music too. Parties. Celebrations. Catering.

Fun.

But now this Tudor-style home in Bel Air is tense. Those that live here are worn. Nervous. They are doing their best, but the pressure is intolerable, the demands not to be believed. They are suffering the agonizing results of bad judgment. Faulty figuring. Sour deals.

They have misread the general public.

There was a time when that seemed impossible. When Mr. and Mrs. Alan T. were riding high. The smartest, the sharpest producing and packaging team in town. Sure-footed, never faltering, never a mistake. Residuals, big box office, percentages of the gross, not the net. It all belonged to Mr. and Mrs. Alan T. Their respective fingers on the pulse of America. Mr. and Mrs. Right Place at the Right Time. There with the goods. Disaffected youth when America wanted disaffected youth. Black exploitation. Nostalgia. Male bonding. The occult. They predicted every single trend. Right on the money. Time after time. They had contacts. They had respect. They had power. They had four brand-new leased Mercedes all at once. Chocolate brown. Off-white. Silver gray. Deepest maroon. All paid for, compliments of the studio.

Then it all started caving in on them. A mistake here, an error there. Little things at first: going into general release too soon; giving a twenty-year-old director a budget he couldn't handle; using an editor with a drinking problem;

putting a cute little number in a role that swamped her. Bad reviews. Drive-in city.

The maroon was the first to go. Then the off-white. Mr. and Mrs. Alan T. live with the sort of despair that few of us can truly understand. They are like wounded deer, like victims of some corrosive disease of the soul. They sit and stare at each other in mournful silence. They know it is only a matter of time. They know the silver gray is next. Then even the chocolate brown will be gone. They castigate themselves and each other. Their plight is all the harder to bear, for these once proud people see it as a failing of their own. An unrelenting self-induced horror.

Mr. and Mrs. Alan T. missed the boat on science fiction.

How it happened they simply cannot imagine. All the signs were there: paperbacks selling like hotcakes; huge conventions of future buffs; comic books; toys. A trend about to be. A gold mine. A money machine. A whole new ball game. And where were they? They answer their own question with a horrifying combination of grief and self-loathing. Off on location with some bomb about a Yorkshire terrier possessed by the devil. Yesterday's newspapers, January's Playmate of the Month in February.

Can you come to their aid? Can you help Mr. and Mrs. Alan T.? Try. Please. Make them an offer. They can hardly refuse. Can they?

Kimberly M.

Kimberly M. stands alone in the airline terminal. A solitary figure. Staring as the empty luggage carrousel goes round and round. She knows it is to no avail. She has been there for hours. She has waited. She has talked to them all: the representatives, the ground crew, even, in her blinding panic, the stewardesses. She has had her hopes lifted only to be dashed. Her luggage, she knows, is gone. All seven pieces. All a gift from her grandmother. All Louis Vuitton. All the old stuff. The real stuff.

When it was still leather.

She cannot quite believe this is happening to *her*. It must be some dreadful nightmare from which she will soon awake. It cannot be real. But as Kimberly M. hears the metallic voice announcing the delays and cancellations, she knows this is no hallucination, no dream. They have indeed lost her luggage. Where it is she hasn't a clue. Taken by mistake? In a taxi on its way back to town? En route to Cleveland? Checked through to Hong Kong? She may never know.

Gone, her Sonia Rykiel sweaters. Her favorite Kenzo shirt. Gone, her new supply of Clinique. Her Maud Frizon shoes. Gone, her Charles Jourdan boots. Gone, her address book. Yes. Her address book. Gone. Gone. Gone.

Kimberly M. stands alone in the airline terminal. A solitary figure. Staring as the empty luggage carrousel goes round and round.

Kimberly M. has lost her luggage. Certainly you can spare some of your own.

REMEMBER THE GREEDIEST!

PARENTAL GUIDANCE

*A*s the title suggests, this piece is intended for those among us who have taken on the job of human reproduction. And while I am not unmindful of the fact that many of my readers are familiar with the act of reproduction only insofar as it applies to a too-recently fabricated Louis XV armoire, I nevertheless feel that certain things cannot be left unsaid. For although distinctly childless myself, I find that I am possessed of some fairly strong opinions on the subject of the rearing of the young. The reasons for this are varied, not to say rococo, and range from genuine concern for the future of mankind to simple, cosmetic disdain.

Being a good deal less villainous than is popularly supposed, I do not hold small children entirely accountable for their own behavior. By and large, I feel that this burden must be borne by their elders. Therefore, in an effort to make knowledge power, I offer the following suggestions:

Your responsibility as a parent is not as great as you might imagine. You need not supply the world with the next conqueror of disease or major motion-picture star. If your child simply grows up to be someone who does not use the word "collectible" as a noun, you can consider yourself an unqualified success.

———

Children do not really need money. After all, they don't have to pay rent or send mailgrams. Therefore their allowance should be just large enough to cover chewing gum and an occasional pack of cigarettes. A child with his own savings account and/or tax shelter is not going to be a child who scares easy.

———

A child who is not rigorously instructed in the matter of table manners is a child whose future is being dealt with cavalierly. A person who makes an admiral's hat out of a linen napkin is not going to be in wild social demand.

———

The term "child actor" is redundant. He should not be further incited.

———

Do not have your child's hair cut by a real hairdresser in a real hairdressing salon. He is, at this point, far too short to be exposed to contempt.

———

Do not, on a rainy day, ask your child what he feels like doing, because I assure you that what he feels like doing, you won't feel like watching.

———

Educational television should be absolutely forbidden. It can only lead to unreasonable expectations and eventual disappointment when your child discovers that the letters of the alphabet do not leap up out of books and dance around the room with royal-blue chickens.

———

If you are truly serious about preparing your child for the future, don't teach him to subtract—teach him to deduct.

———

Make every effort to avoid ostentatiously Biblical names. Nothing will show your hand more.

———

Do not send your child to the sort of progressive school that permits writing on the walls unless you want him to grow up to be TAKI 183.

———

If you must give your child lessons, send him to driving school. He is far more likely to end up owning a Datsun than he is a Stradivarius.

———

Designer clothes worn by children are like snowsuits worn by adults. Few can carry it off successfully.

———

Never allow your child to call you by your first name. He hasn't known you long enough.

———

Do not encourage your child to express himself artistically unless you are George Balanchine's mother.

———

Do not elicit your child's political opinions. He doesn't know any more than you do.

———

Do not allow your children to mix drinks. It is unseemly and they use too much vermouth.

———

Letting your child choose his own bedroom furniture is like letting your dog choose his own veterinarian.

———

Your child is watching too much television if there exists the possibility that he might melt down.

———

Don't bother discussing sex with small children. They rarely have anything to add.

———

Never, for effect, pull a gun on a small child. He won't get it.

———

Ask your child what he wants for dinner only if he's buying.

———

TIPS FOR TEENS

T here is perhaps, for all concerned, no period of life so unpleasant, so unappealing, so downright unpalatable, as that of adolescence. And while pretty much everyone who comes into contact with him is disagreeably affected, certainly no one is in for a ruder shock than the actual teenager himself. Fresh from twelve straight years of uninterrupted cuteness, he is singularly unprepared to deal with the harsh consequences of inadequate personal appearance. Almost immediately upon entering the thirteenth year of life, a chubby little child becomes a big fat girl, and a boy previously spoken of as "small for his age" finds that he is, in reality, a boy who is short.

Problems of physical beauty, grave though they be, are not all that beset the unwary teen. Philosophical, spiritual, social, legal—a veritable multitude of difficulties daily confront him. Understandably disconcerted, the teenager almost invariably finds himself in a state of unrelenting misery. This is, of course, unfortunate, even lamentable. Yet one frequently discovers a lack of sympathy for the troubled youth. This dearth of compassion is undoubtedly due to the teenager's insistence upon dealing with his lot in an unduly boisterous fashion. He is, quite simply, at an age where he can keep nothing to himself. No impulse too fleeting, no sentiment too raw, that the teenager does not feel compelled to share it with those around him.

This sort of behavior naturally tends to have an alienating effect. And while this is oftimes its major intent, one cannot help but respond with hearty ill will.

Therefore, in the interest of encouraging if not greater understanding, at least greater decorum, I have set down the following words of advice.

If in addition to being physically unattractive you find that you do not get along well with others, do not under any circumstances attempt to alleviate this situation by developing an interesting personality. An interesting personality is, in an adult, insufferable. In a teenager it is frequently punishable by law.

———

Wearing dark glasses at the breakfast table is socially acceptable only if you are legally blind or partaking of your morning meal out of doors during a total eclipse of the sun.

———

Should your political opinions be at extreme variance with those of your parents, keep in mind that while it is indeed your constitutional right to express these sentiments verbally, it is unseemly to do so with your mouth full—particularly when it is full of the oppressor's standing rib roast.

———

Think before you speak. Read before you think. This will give you something to think about that you didn't make up yourself—a wise move at any age, but most especially at seventeen, when you are in the greatest danger of coming to annoying conclusions.

———

Try to derive some comfort from the knowledge that if your guidance counselor were working up to *his* potential, he wouldn't still be in high school.

———

The teen years are fraught with any number of hazards, but none so perilous as that which manifests itself as a tendency to consider movies an important art form. If you are presently, or just about to be, of this opinion, perhaps I can spare you years of unbearable pretension by posing this question: If movies (or films, as you are probably now referring to them) were of such a high and serious nature, can you possibly entertain even the slightest notion that they would show them in a place that sold Orange Crush and Jujubes?

———

It is at this point in your life that you will be giving the greatest amount of time and attention to matters of sex. This not only is acceptable, but should, in fact, be encouraged, for this is the last time that sex will be genuinely exciting. The more farsighted among you may wish to cultivate supplementary interests in order that you might have something to do when you get older. I personally recommend the smoking of cigarettes—a habit with staying power.

———

While we're on the subject of cigarettes, do not forget that adolescence is also the last time that you can reasonably expect to be forgiven a taste for a brand that might by way of exotic shape, color or package excite comment.

———

The girl in your class who suggests that this year the Drama Club put on *The Bald Soprano* will be a thorn in people's sides all of her life.

―――――

Should you be a teenager blessed with uncommon good looks, document this state of affairs by the taking of photographs. It is the only way anyone will ever believe you in years to come.

―――――

Avoid the use of drugs whenever possible. For while they may, at this juncture, provide a pleasant diversion, they are, on the whole, not the sort of thing that will in later years (should you *have* later years) be of much use in the acquisition of richly rewarding tax shelters and beachfront property.

―――――

If you reside in a state where you attain your legal majority while still in your teens, pretend that you don't. There isn't an adult alive who would want to be contractually bound by a decision he came to at the age of nineteen.

―――――

Remember that as a teenager you are at the last stage in your life when you will be happy to hear that the phone is for you.

―――――

Stand firm in your refusal to remain conscious during algebra. In real life, I assure you, there is no such thing as algebra.

―――――

AT HOME WITH POPE RON

*I*t is a clear, crisp day, the sunlight glinting brilliantly off the spires of St. Peter's Basilica—the entire scene as impressive and monumental as ever—but I scarcely notice as I make my hurried way across the square, for I am late for my interview and as any good journalist knows, popes don't like to be kept waiting. I enter the Vatican breathlessly, take quick note of the really quite attractive Swiss Guard and make my way to the papal apartments, where I am to meet the man who has arranged this interview—the cardinal bishop closest to the pope.

"Hi," says a tall, rather lanky fellow whom I would place in his very early thirties, "I'm Jeff Cardinal Lucas, but call me Jeff." Jeff extends a friendly hand and I, not being a Catholic, am somewhat at a loss as to what to do. Just then I am rescued from what could easily have turned into an extremely embarrassing situation, by a husky masculine voice. "Jeff, Jeff, if that's the girl from the magazine, tell her I'll be with her in a minute. I'm just finishing up an encyclical."

True to his word, sixty seconds later I am confronted by a tall, somewhat shaggy-haired man with startlingly long eyelashes and a ready, even impish, grin. "Hi," he says in that hauntingly deep voice that I had heard only a minute before. "I'm the Supreme Pontiff, but call me Ron—everyone does."

And much to my surprise I do, and *easily,* for Pope Ron's genuine warmth is infectious. Soon we are sitting comfortably on a big, old, leather sofa chatting away as if we had known each other forever. Before too long, we are joined by Sue, the pope's delicate blond wife of the pre-Raphaelite curls and long, tapering fingers, and Dylan, Ron's boyish little son from his first marriage.

I check my tape recorder to make sure it's working and ask Ron if he would like to start by telling me a little about his personal life, what he does to relax—to escape from the pressures of holiness and infallibility.

"Well," says Ron, "I would first like to say that this is, after all, the new Church and things have really loosened up around here. I mean, I do try to adapt to others. To understand and consider points of view different from my own. To grow. To extend myself. To explore the various regions of thought. You know, I have kind of a motto that I found to be of tremendous use to me in this job. A motto that I think has done a lot to make the Church really relevant. In fact, Sue here liked it so much that she made me this." Ron divests himself of his robe and reveals a white cotton T-shirt emblazoned in red with the legend INFALLIBLE BUT NOT INFLEXIBLE. "Of course," continued the pontiff, "this is just the prototype. As soon as Sue is finished with the urn she's working on now—you know, of course, that she's really incredible with the potter's wheel—she's going to see about having them made up for the entire Sacred College of Cardinals.

"As for relaxation, well, one of the things I really like to do is work with my hands. I mean, it really humbles a man, even a pope, to have tactile contact with the raw materials of nature. See that scepter over there? It took me six months to carve it out of rosewood, but it was worth it because by making it myself I feel that it's really a part of me, really mine." At this, Sue smiles proudly and gives Ron's ring a playful little kiss. It is easy to see what a terribly *happy* couple they are.

"I do other things too, things around the palace. Sue and I do them together, and even Dylan helps, don't you, Dyl?" Ron asks paternally as he rumples his young son's hair. "I mean, when we first moved in here you wouldn't have believed it. Incredibly formal, incredibly elaborate, unbelievably uptight. And it's such a big place really that we've barely made a dent. But one thing we have done—finished just last week, as a matter of fact, I mean Sue and I together, of course—was that we took the walls of the Sistine Chapel down to the natural brick, and now it really looks great, really warm, really basic."

We sip a little mint tea, and watch with amusement as little Dylan tries on his father's miter. I join in the gentle laughter as the large headdress falls over his little face. "Now for my next question, Ron, and I know you'll answer me honestly, I mean that goes without saying. Is the pope Catholic?"

"Look," he says, "if you mean me specifically, I mean me *personally*, yes, I am Catholic. But you know, of course, that this old bugaboo is no longer really applicable. The field is definitely opening up, and being Catholic really didn't swing

my election as pope. The Sacred College of Cardinals looks
for someone open to God, someone at home with his or her
own feelings, someone, you might say, who can communi-
cate rather than just excommunicate—which is, after all, so
negative, so the opposite of the type of actualization that I
hope the Church now represents. Yes, the Church is opening up to every possibility, and I see no reason why we can't
expect in the not-too-distant future a Pope Rochester, a
Pope Ellen, even a Pope Ira."

"Pope Ira?" I ask. "Isn't that a bit unlikely? A Jewish
pope after the long Church history of saying that the Jews
killed Christ?"

"Look," Ron pontificates, "what's past is past. You know
we no longer blame the death of Christ on the Jews. I mean,
obviously they were involved, but you have to look at things
historically and nowadays the Church accepts the bull that
I issued last year which decreed an acceptance of the fact
that all they probably did was just hassle him, and that's
what my bull decreed; the Jews *hassled* Christ, they didn't
actually kill him."

Much relieved, I ask Ron about the early years, the struggle years, the tough years that every young man with scep-
ters in his eyes must endure—nay, must triumph over—if
he is to reach his lordly goal.

"Yeah," says Ron, "it was rough, real rough, but it was
fun too. I mean, I've done the whole thing, really gone the
distance, from altar boy to the Big P. I've been there in the
confessional listening to the little boys tell of impure
thoughts. I've been there baptizing the babies—upfront so
to speak." He chuckles softly at his own joke. "I've run the
bingo games, married the faithful, tended the flock. I was
the youngest cardinal ever to come out of the Five Towns,

and it wasn't always easy, but I've had some laughs along the way and it was all worthwhile the night they elected me pope. I remember that night. It was warm and breezy and Pam and I—Pam was my first wife—stood together watching the smoke, waiting and waiting. Nine times, but it seemed like a million, until the smoke was white and I heard I'd made it. Jesus, it was beautiful, really beautiful."

Ron brushes away the tears that sentiment has evoked, but he is obviously unashamed of real emotion, free from the repression that has so long constrained men. I mention this and Ron is pleased, even grateful, that I have noticed his supremacy over the old, uptight values that deny men the right to their feelings.

"Look," he says dogmatically, and it is easy to see that the papacy has not been wasted on this man, "we're all in this together, you know—I mean, Sue and I are *partners.* We discuss everything, and I mean everything. I wouldn't consider issuing an edict without discussing it with her first. Not because she's my wife, but because I respect her opinion; I value her judgment. Lots of things she does on her own, like instituting the whole-grain host. I mean, that was *totally* her thing. It was *she* who pointed out to *me* that for years the faithful had been poisoning their systems with overly refined hosts. And that was only *one* of the things she's done. There are hundreds—I couldn't possibly name them all. Yeah, Sue is really something else. I mean, she has definitely got the interests of the faithful at heart. You've got to believe me when I say she's thinking of others all the time. She's not just my lady, man; she's *our* lady. And you can take it from me that that's no bull, that's strictly from the heart."

THE MODERN-DAY LIVES OF THE SAINTS

ST. GARRETT THE PETULANT (died 1974): Patron of make-up artists, invoked against puffiness and uneven skin tone.

Garrett was born in Cleveland in 1955, or so he claimed. His father was a factory worker who took little interest in his pale, delicate son. His mother, a pious woman who supplemented the family income by selling cosmetics door-to-door, was perhaps Garrett's earthly inspiration.

From the time he was a very small child Garrett exhibited an almost precocious generosity of spirit, and was constantly volunteering to do "at least the eyes" of those females with whom he came in contact. At the age of eleven, clad only in rayon, he walked forty-seven miles in a terrible blizzard in order to place in the deepest forest an offering of food for the woodland creatures. The site of this blessed action is now often visited by pilgrims from all over the world, and is known as Cherries in the Snow. It was also around this time that Garrett performed his first miracle by correcting the appearance of a local matron's broad and fleshy nose without the visible use of contouring powder.

In the summer of his sixteenth year Garrett met a visiting New York stage actor in the Greyhound bus station, and it was through the kind offices of this man (whose own deep sense of humility has led him to request anonymity) that Garrett had his first great revlonation. Spent and trembling, he saw before him a large reflective surface surrounded by shining lights. He saw needful, begging eyes. He saw undefined cheekbones. He saw dry, parched lips. He saw an array of splendid colors. He saw his destiny.

Much inspired by Garrett's way, the actor assisted him in his journey to the city of New York. Here Garrett performed his second miracle by purchasing and furnishing a lavish co-op apartment despite the fact that he had no visible means of support.

News quickly spread throughout the city that Garrett was capable of truly amazing transformations. Women who were the recipients of his attentions called him Blessed and he was soon Venerated by all those in the know.

Despite his exalted position Garrett practiced humility and was often to be seen in rough districts of the city behaving in a most submissive manner while performing low and menial services for others. Garrett was found martyred in the bedroom of his East Side penthouse apartment late one Sunday morning.

ST. AMANDA OF NEW YORK, SOUTHAMPTON AND PALM BEACH (died 1971; came out 1951): Patroness of the well-bred, is invoked against the "cut direct," having to dip into capital and improper use of the word "home."

The daughter of Mr. and Mrs. Morgan Hayes Birmingham IV of New York, Southampton and Palm Beach, Amanda was born at Doctors Hospital in New York on January 3, 1933. She made her debut at the Gotham Ball and was a graduate of The Convent of the Sacred Heart and Manhattanville College. Her paternal grandfather, Morgan Hayes Birmingham III, was a member of the New York Stock Exchange and the founder of the firm of Birmingham, Stevens and Ryan. She was a descendant of Colonel Thomas M. Hayes.

Almost from birth it was apparent that Amanda was blessed with an almost sublime sense of tact. During her baptism at St. Ignatius Loyola she was the very picture of infant dignity and neither cried nor wriggled, despite the fact that the attending priest was generally thought to be something of an arriviste. Her childhood was characterized by a nearly fanatical attention to detail, and notice was first taken of her miraculous powers when at the age of three there appeared, appropriately placed about the nursery, Lalique vases filled with perfectly arranged, out-of-season flowers. The second indication of these powers occurred when Amanda, a mere nine years old, managed to correct, while dutifully attending her French class in New York, an extraordinarily indelicate seating plan committed by her maternal grandmother's social secretary in Hobe Sound.

Amanda's martyrdom took place during a weekend house party when she knowingly allowed herself to be served, *from the right,* a salad containing wild mushrooms picked by her host, rather than strike an unpleasant note by refusing.

ST. WAYNE (died circa 1975): Patron of middle children, invoked against whatever's left over.

Wayne was born two years after his brilliant and handsome brother Mike and three and a half years before his perfectly adorable sister Jane. Very little is remembered of his life and works, if any, and his canonization is the result of a unique mix-up in which Mike was made a saint twice and with typical generosity gave Wayne his extra sainthood.

ST. INGMAR-FRANÇOIS-JEAN-JONAS-ANDREW: Patron of graduate film students, invoked against going to the movies for fun, detractors of Stan Brakhage and disbelievers in the genius of John Ford.

St. Ingmar-François-Jean-Jonas-Andrew was born in a starkly lit delivery room in the kind of small American town that is all small American towns. From infancy he was astonishingly perceptive, and invariably saw layers of meaning not apparent to the average moviegoer. As early as his sixth birthday Ingmar-François-Jean-Jonas-Andrew displayed the remarkable dual tendency to overwrite and underexplain.

Among the many miracles to his credit are getting adults to actually attend a Jerry Lewis Film Festival and introducing a course at an accredited university entitled "The Philosophy of Busby Berkeley and Its Influence on Rainer Werner Fassbinder and Robert Bresson."

Rather than martyr himself, St. Ingmar-François-Jean-Jonas-Andrew sent one of his students.

THE SERVANT PROBLEM

*I*t was just a few years ago that, owing to some rather favorable publicity, I came into what is known as a little money. This unexpected but most welcome piece of good fortune enabled me for the very first time to secure living quarters that one could, if pressed, describe as commodious. I promptly set out to fix the place up, and soon acquired some dandy home furnishings carefully chosen to give a false impression of both my breeding and my background. Surrounded by these venerable objects, I cheerfully noted that I had at long last achieved all three of my material goals: new money, old furniture and a separate room to write in.

Due, however, to my unhappy penchant for whiling away the hours (not to mention years) reading other people's books, I was soon in possession of what looked very much indeed like six small public libraries wherein smoking was not merely allowed but actually, and even brutally, enforced. Ashes to ashes, dust to dust. Were truer words ever spoken? I think not. There was no question about it, I needed a maid, and needed one badly. Unfortunately, I had not the slightest idea of how to go about getting one. This worried me enormously. I became flustered, then agitated, until finally I was compelled to take myself in hand and explain to myself calmly yet firmly that a maid was not, after all, the world's most exotic prize, and could undoubtedly be procured in a perfectly ordinary fashion. A couple of perfectly ordinary fashions came to mind but were shortly discounted. A store? No, it had been years since you could buy a maid, and even then, not in stores. A bar? Don't be ridiculous. I was looking for a maid, not an agent. Where then? I was, it seemed, stymied, stuck, stopped dead in my tracks, no place to go, nowhere to turn. Nowhere to turn, that is, until I fortuitously recalled a friend who had come into *her* money by accident of birth rather than by dint of hard work. Here was the very person to advise me, to smooth my path, to show me the way.

I quickly telephoned her and evidently displayed my ignorance to such great advantage that she agreed not only to help out but to actually get up a small group of likely candidates. She regretted, however, that since I was looking for someone to come only one day a week, I could not expect the sort of high-quality service that was routinely available on her own premises. I took this news admirably and awaited further instructions. A few days later she called to announce that she was sending over some possibilities for me to interview—and by interview, she stressed, she did not mean asking them where they got their ideas or if they had always been funny, but rather, where else they were employed, how much they charged and exactly what duties they were willing to perform. I was then to decide if I liked them—*as maids, not people.* She emphasized this not only as if the two were mutually exclusive but also in a tone of voice that I felt to be unduly withering. When I expressed these sentiments, she replied that she was merely cautioning me against imposing personal standards inappropriate to the situation. By this she apparently meant that you decided you liked a maid because she ironed, and not because she recognized you from being on the *Today* show. It was at this juncture that I began to suspect that having a maid might not be the fun it looked. Nevertheless, I persevered and agreed to begin the interviewing process immediately.

Later that same afternoon, the first applicant arrived in the form of an excessively well-groomed young man. Modern-day life, it seems, has given us not only girl ministers but also boy maids. I am in favor of neither, but seeing as how he was already standing there I let him in and politely offered to take his sweater. He declined, presumably because he didn't want to go to all the trouble of untying it. I attempted to lead him down the hall, but as we passed the bedroom something caught his eye and he wandered in to take a closer look. His attention had been captured by a small painting that hung over the fireplace.

"Decorative art," he stated. "I suppose you find it amusing."

"No," I replied, wondering how many times I had met this boy before, "I find it decorative."

"The bed?" he inquired with a lift of one eyebrow.

"Renaissance Revival," I parried—then thrust. "Attributed to Herter."

"Ah," he said, "American."

The interview, as far as I was concerned, was over. If he didn't dust American furniture there was little chance he did windows. Before, however, I could advise him of this, he had made his way into the living room, where I found him a moment later decoratively draped across my American sofa. He looked up as I entered, smiled graciously, and with an expressive little nod of his expressive little head, indicated that I might be seated. He then treated me to a lengthy monologue, the purpose of which was to acquaint me with his seriously rarefied sensibility. During the course of this, I tried several times to ask him how much he charged, having earlier hit upon the plan of hastening his leave-taking by offering him a highly minimum wage. But every time I raised the subject he deflected it. Obviously, he considered any discussion of money to be vulgar, tasteless and shockingly parvenu. Finally he stooped to breathe, and I inquired softly if perhaps rather than being paid he wouldn't just prefer that I quietly make a contribution to his favorite charity. This, so to speak, did the trick, and he left with no further fanfare.

Victory was mine to savor but briefly, for I had yet before me a seemingly endless procession of aspiring domestics. So unanimous were they in their two most untenable demands that with fair rapidity they became one big blur. Without exception, they insisted on coming to work during the day, and furthermore made it clear that they had every intention of coming to the house. I was loath, of course, to meet these stipulations, since during the day I am home not writing. During the night I am *out* not writing, and this, obviously, was the most convenient arrangement. I was, however, singularly unsuccessful in persuading any of them of this, and was eventually forced to choose the best of a bad and deplorably illogical lot. Ever mindful of my friend's advice, I picked the one that I liked best as a maid, and while the fact that she ironed most assuredly contributed to my feelings of affection, the fact that she spoke not a single word of English is, I must confess, what clinched the deal. If I was going to have to spend the entire day in the company of another, I most certainly preferred another who had not even the vaguest notion of what I was saying on the telephone.

The first few times she came we coexisted peacefully, if not lovingly, but by the fourth week I began to find the situation intolerable. Although I made every effort to stay out of her way, she was forever following me from room to room brandishing dangerous-looking household appliances and looking at me contemptuously in Portuguese. It was all too apparent that she had very little use for a person who, it seemed, spent all day long lying around the house using up towels and talking on the telephone in a foreign language. After one episode involving a particularly vigorous and disdainful emptying of ashtrays, I accepted the fact that henceforth I would be obliged to spend my day out of doors.

At first, going out during the day was kind of interesting. A lot of places were open, and it was undeniably well lit, though rather crowded and a tad noisy. I did my level best to if not enjoy, then at least to adapt myself. Soon, however, the novelty wore off, and I found it increasingly difficult to pursue my normal way of life in this alien and hostile environment. I was repeatedly harassed and ofttimes insulted by surly doormen who did not smile upon me fondly as I lolled about beneath their canopies, minding my own business and doing the *TV Guide* crossword puzzle. Crowds gathered and trouble brewed as I attempted to keep in touch with a wide circle of friends via public phone. And time after time

I was the innocent recipient of pointed remarks as I caught up on my reading while attractively posed atop the hoods of other people's parked cars.

Clearly, this could not go on forever; something had to be done, and fast. There were, of course, no easy answers. The problem was a serious one and demanded a serious effort if it was ever to be solved. To this end I was fully prepared to use every possible method at my disposal. Unfortunately, however, the possible methods at my disposal are rarely those involving careful research and painstaking detail. They tend, it is true, more in the direction of harebrained schemes and crackpot theories. In view of this, it is understandable that I was, in the end, unable to come to any firm resolution and can offer only the tangible written proof that I tried.

THE TANGIBLE WRITTEN PROOF THAT I TRIED

It was apparent to me that an apartment, like a sweater, was impossible to clean if one was in it. Following this logic, it was then equally apparent that an apartment, like a sweater, should be sent out to be cleaned. I decided that this could be accomplished by the general establishment of stores for this purpose. So far, so good. The kinks in this thing didn't show up until I came to the part where one went to pick up the apartment. It was at this point that I remembered the dirty-sweater analogy, and my heart sank. This sensation was simultaneously accompanied by a vision of myself standing at a counter screaming, "This is not my apartment! Don't you think I know what my own apartment looks like? Mine was the one with the separate room to write in and the two wood-burning fireplaces. This apartment is not mine. This apartment has no separate room to write in, only one wood-burning fireplace and a loft bed. Believe me, I don't have a loft bed. That I promise you. So don't tell me that this is my apartment, it's just that the rest of it didn't come back yet. And do you mind telling me how you could lose a wood-burning fireplace? *It was not hanging by a thread.* It was attached to a very substantial plaster wall. This isn't my apartment and I'm not taking it. No, I wouldn't rather have this apartment than no apartment at all. I want *my* apartment, the one I brought you. All right, I will—I *will* sue you. Don't think I won't. You'll hear from my lawyer. I'm going to call him right now."

And with that I saw myself turning on my heel and angrily stalking out. Lamentably, the next thing I saw was myself back outside, in a public phone booth with crowds gathering and trouble brewing. It was then that I decided that if I was going to have to make my phone calls outside anyway, I might as well keep both fireplaces.

THINGS

THINGS

All of the things in the world can be divided into two basic categories: natural things and artificial things. Or, as they are more familiarly known, nature and art. Now, nature, as I am only too well aware, has her enthusiasts, but on the whole, I am not to be counted among them. To put it rather bluntly, I am not the type who wants to go back to the land; I am the type who wants to go back to the hotel. This state of affairs is at least partially due to the fact that nature and I have so little in common. We don't go to the same restaurants, laugh at the same jokes or, most significant, see the same people.

This was not, however, always the case. As a child I was frequently to be found in a natural setting: playing in the snow, walking in the woods, wading in the pond. All these things were standard events in my daily life. But little by little I grew up, and it was during this process of maturation that I began to notice some of nature's more glaring deficiencies. First of all, nature is by and large to be found out of doors, a location where, it cannot be argued, there are never enough comfortable chairs. Secondly, for fully half of the time it is day out there, a situation created by just the sort of harsh overhead lighting that is so unflattering to the heavy smoker. Lastly, and most pertinent to this discourse, is the fact that natural things are by their very definition wild, unkempt and more often than not crawling with bugs. Quite obviously, then, natural things are just the kind of things that one does not strive to acquire. *Objets d'art* are one thing; *objets d'nature* are not. Who, after all, could possibly want to own something that even the French don't have a word for?

In view of all this I have prepared a little chart designed to more graphically illustrate the vast superiority of that which is manufactured over that which is not.

NATURE	ART
The sun	The toaster oven
Your own two feet	Your own two Bentleys
Windfall apples	Windfall profits
Roots and berries	Linguini with clam sauce
Time marching on	The seven-second delay
Milk	Butter
The good earth	25 percent of the gross
Wheat	Linguini with clam sauce
A man for all seasons	Marc Bohan for Dior
Ice	Ice cubes
Facial hair	Razor blades
The smell of the country-side after a long, soaking rain	Linguini with clam sauce
TB	TV
The mills of God	Roulette
A tinkling mountain brook	Paris

Now that you have had an opportunity to gain an overview of the subject, it is time to explore things more thoroughly, time to ask yourselves what you have learned and how you can best apply your new-found knowledge. Well, obviously, the first and most important thing you have learned is that linguini with clam sauce is mankind's crowning achievement. But as this is a concept readily grasped, it is unnecessary to linger over it or discuss it in greater detail.

As to the question of how you can best apply what you have learned, I believe that it would be highly beneficial to you all were we to examine the conventional wisdom on the subject of things in order to see what it looks like in the light of your new-found knowledge:

THE CONVENTIONAL WISDOM ON THE SUBJECT OF
THINGS AS SEEN IN THE LIGHT OF YOUR NEW-FOUND
KNOWLEDGE

All good things come to those who wait. This is a concept that parallels in many respects another well-known thought, that of the meek inheriting the earth. With that in mind, let us use a time-honored method of education and break the first statement into its two major component parts: a) All good things; b) come to those who wait. Immediately it is apparent that thanks to our previous study we are well informed as to which exactly the good things are. It is when we come to "those who wait" that we are entering virgin territory. Educators have found that in cases like this it is often best to use examples from actual life. So then, we must think of a place that from our own experience we know as a place where "those who wait" might, in fact, be waiting.

Thus I feel that the baggage claim area of a large metropolitan airport might well serve our purpose.

Now, in addressing the fundamental issue implied by this question—i.e., the veracity of the statement "All good things come to those who wait"—we are in actuality asking the question, "Do, in fact, all good things come to those who wait?" In breaking our answer into *its* two major component parts, we find that we know that: a) among "all good things" are to be found linguini with clam sauce, the Bentley automobile and the ever-fascinating city of Paris.

We also know that: b) "those who wait" are waiting at O'Hare. We then think back to our own real-life adventures, make one final check of our helpful chart and are sadly compelled to conclude that "No, all good things do *not* come to those who wait"—unless due to unforeseeably personal preferences on the part of "those who wait," "all good things" are discovered to include an item entitled SOME OF YOUR LUGGAGE MISSING ALL OF ITS CONTENTS.

A thing of beauty is a joy forever: this graceful line from a poem written by John Keats is not so much inaccurate as it is archaic. Mr. Keats, it must be remembered, was not only a poet but also a product of the era in which he lived. Additionally, it must not be forgotten that one of the salient features of the early nineteenth century was an inordinate admiration for the simple ability to endure. Therefore, while a thing of beauty is a joy, to be sure, we of the modern age, confined no longer by outmoded values, are free to acknowledge that nine times out of ten a weekend is long enough.

Each man kills the thing he loves: and understandably so, when he has been led to believe that it will be a joy forever.

Doing your own thing: the use of the word "thing" in this context is unusually precise, since those who are prone to this expression actually do *do* things as opposed to those who do work—i.e., pottery is a thing—writing is a work.

Life is just one damned thing after another: and death is a cabaret.

POINTERS FOR PETS

I feel compelled by duty to begin this discourse with what I actually think of as a statement, but what will more probably be construed as an admission. I do not like animals. Of any sort. I don't even like the idea of animals. Animals are no friends of mine. They are not welcome in my house. They occupy no space in my heart. Animals are off my list. I will say, however, in the spirit of qualification, that I mean them no particular harm. I won't bother animals if animals won't bother me. Well, perhaps I had better amend that last sentence. I won't *personally* bother animals. I do feel, though, that a plate bereft of a good cut of something rare is an affront to the serious diner, and that while I have frequently run across the fellow who could, indeed, be described as a broccoli-and-potatoes man, I cannot say that I have ever really taken to such a person.

Therefore, I might more accurately state that I do not like animals, with two exceptions. The first being in the past tense, at which point I like them just fine, in the form of nice crispy spareribs and Bass Weejun penny loafers. And the second being outside, by which I mean not merely outside, as in outside the house, but genuinely outside, as in outside in the woods, or preferably outside in the South American jungle. This is, after all, only fair. I don't go there; why should they come here?

The above being the case, it should then come as no surprise that I do not approve of the practice of keeping animals as pets. "Not approve" is too mild: pets should be disallowed by law. Especially dogs. Especially in New York City.

I have not infrequently verbalized this sentiment in what now passes for polite society, and have invariably been the recipient of the information that even if dogs should be withheld from the frivolous, there would still be the blind and the pathologically lonely to think of. I am not totally devoid of compassion, and after much thought I believe that I have hit upon the perfect solution to this problem: let the lonely lead the blind. The implementation of this plan would provide companionship to one and a sense of direction to the other, without inflicting on the rest of the populace the all too common spectacle of grown men addressing German shepherds in the respectful tones best reserved for elderly clergymen and Internal Revenue agents.

You animal lovers uninterested in helping news dealers across busy intersections will just have to seek companionship elsewhere. If actual friends are not within your grasp, may I suggest that you take a cue from your favorite celebrity and consider investing in a really good entourage. The advantages of such a scheme are inestimable: an entourage is indisputably superior to a dog (or even, of course, actual friends), and will begin to pay for itself almost immediately. You do not have to walk an entourage; on the contrary, one of the major functions of an entourage is that *it* walks *you*.

You do not have to name an entourage. You do not have to play with an entourage. You do not have to take an entourage to the vet—although the conscientious entourage owner makes certain that his entourage has had all of its shots. You do, of course, have to feed an entourage, but this can be accomplished in decent Italian restaurants and without the bother and mess of large tin cans and special plastic dishes.

If the entourage suggestion does not appeal to you, perhaps you should alter your concept of companionship. Living things need not enter into it at all. Georgian silver and Duncan Phyfe sofas make wonderful companions, as do all alcoholic beverages and out-of-season fruits. Use your imagination, study up on the subject. You'll think of something.

If, however, you do not think of something—and animal lovers being a singularly intractable lot, chances are that you won't—I have decided to direct the remainder of my remarks to the pets themselves in the hope that they might at least learn to disport themselves with dignity and grace.

If you are a dog and your owner suggests that you wear a sweater . . . suggest that he wear a tail.

———

If you have been named after a human being of artistic note, run away from home. It is unthinkable that even an animal should be obliged to share quarters with anyone who calls a cat Ford Madox Ford.

———

Dogs who earn their living by appearing in television commercials in which they constantly and aggressively demand meat should remember that in at least one Far Eastern country they *are* meat.

———

If you are only a bird in a gilded cage—count your blessings.

———

A dog who thinks he is man's best friend is a dog who obviously has never met a tax lawyer.

———

If you are an owl being kept as a pet, I applaud and encourage your tendency to hoot. You are to be highly commended for expressing such a sentiment. An owl is, of course, not a pet at all; it is an unforgivable and wistful effort in the direction of whimsy.

———

No animal should ever jump up on the dining-room furniture unless absolutely certain that he can hold his own in the conversation.

———

THE FRANCE*S* ANN LEBOWITZ COLLECTION

Following are a few selected pages from the forthcoming auction catalogue of the estate of Frances
Ann Lebowitz.

Length 19 inches (48 cm)

See illustration.

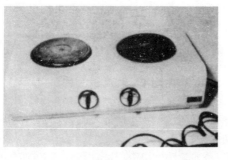

1. KORD (BRAND NAME)

Thus is inscribed this important example of popularly priced
hot plate. White enameled metal with black brand-name
inscription and dials, this two-burner plate was personally

delivered to its present owner by Mr. Roper, the absentee building superintendent long thought to be a mythical figure. While actual physical manifestation of Mr. Roper is of keen interest to those scholars and collectors dedicated to a more detailed and esoteric study of *Memento Pori,* or *Reminders of Poverty,* it should be noted that his appearance was a singular one and that he himself is not offered with this lot.

The Kord, however, replaced an earlier hot plate widely believed to have been formerly owned (and used) by all of Mr. Roper's antecedents.

The Kord is interestingly proportioned, featuring two burners but lacking room for two pans. This feature possibly derives from the landlord's insistence on thematic discomfort.

The Frances Ann Lebowitz Collection, one of the largest ever assembled (in an apartment of that size) of *Memento Pori* effectively chronicles man's reaction to having no money from the end of the nineteen-sixties, through latter-nineteen-seventies acquisitions, until the present day.

All artistic media are represented: carvings in furniture, impressions in wall paint, and works in many metal alloys.

To explore all the various moods and historic events that influenced the creation of these objects would be a lengthy task. Some are flimsy, some jerry-built and others merely outmoded, but all seem to reflect man's underpayment of writers on this earth.

The Kord hot plate with its two burners and two dials reminds us that lack of funds is the ultimate poverty and that there is no way to avoid this fact. Possibly the inscription under each dial states it most clearly: *High, Medium, Low.*

2. BROIL KING TOASTER OVEN
EARLY/LATE NINETEEN-SIXTIES

Emblazoned on one side with the Broil King logo, a sort of crown, and on the other side with the legend "infra red Bake 'N' Broil." Trimmed in black plastic, containing aluminum rack and glasslike window, ornamental wire and plug.

Length 17 inches (43 cm)

See illustration.

3. IMPORTANT ROWE SLEEP-OR-SOFA SOFA BED
SECOND HALF NINETEEN SEVENTY-ONE

Executed in plywood, upholstered with a foam-type substance and covered in brown wide-wale cotton corduroy; mattress in blue, gray and white ticking, black-and-white clothish label (do not remove under penalty of law).

Width: 3 feet (.9 m) (when sofa)
6 feet (1.8 m) (when bed)

See illustration.

4. PRIM ROSE CHINA HAND-PAINTED UNDER GLAZE BY NATIONAL BROTHERHOOD OF OPERATIVE POTTERS NINETEEN THIRTY-NINE?

Once the everyday dairy dishes of Mr. and Mrs. Phillip Splaver of Derby, Connecticut, these dessert and dinner plates were originally acquired at the West End Movie Theater in Bridgeport, Connecticut. Fortuitously (the theater owner was Mr. Splaver's brother-in-law), these outstanding vessels (once part of a complete set) painted with gray, black and red streaks on a field of white, were obtained without the principals being compelled to attend a wearying succession of Dish Nights. *3 pieces.*

Diameters: 10 1/2 inches (26.6 cm)
7 1/2 inches (19 cm)

See illustration.

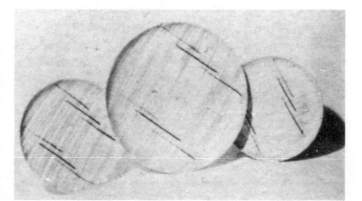

5. GROUP OF SMALL BOXES
   MID-NINETEEN-SEVENTY-EIGHT

The first a red, white and blue cardboard Ambassador tooth-pick box containing many of the original 250 round tooth-picks; two cardboard Gem paper-clip boxes in outstanding shades of green; and a four-color (one an important translu-cent flesh tone) metal box stating contents of three sizes of Johnson & Johnson Band-Aid brand plastic strips. Interest-ing packaging error (lacking juniors). *4 pieces.*

Lengths: 2 3/4 to 3 1/4 inches
(7 to 8.2 cm)

6. THREE ELECTRICAL ALARM CLOCKS,
   ONE OF WHICH WORKS
   LATISH-TWENTIETH-CENTURY

The first two by Westclox (La Salle, Ill.), both lacking "crys-tals" but of interesting design: one almost starkly una-dorned, the other featuring horizontally striped border in tones of tangerine and black. The third a functional time-piece with numerals depicted in a pseudo-iridescent green that very nearly approach trompe l'oeil in that they give every impression of being visible in the dark; amusingly brand-named Lux. *3 pieces.*

Lengths: 3 3/4 to 4 1/4 inches
(9.5 to 11 cm)

See illustration.

7. TYPEWRITER
   TWENTIETH-CENTURY

Remington Rand, gray metal, eleven stuck keys, unwound ribbon; the whole, a mess.

Length 11 inches (28 cm)

See illustration.

8. ANOTHER TYPEWRITER
   TWENTIETH-CENTURY

On loan from generally anonymous art director, lettera DL, two-toned gray metal; neither lot number 7 nor lot number 8 ever used by present owner.

Length 10 inches (25.4 cm)

9. COLLECTION OF FIVE EGGS
   NOT QUITE AS LATE-TWENTIETH-CENTURY
   AS ONE WOULD HAVE HOPED

Representing eggs in two modes, hard-boiled and raw: three of former, two of latter. Together with medium-blue cardboard egg carton and enamel saucepan similarly colored. *5 pieces* (at the moment).

10. PAIR OF INDUSTRIAL QUALITY EARPLUGS
EARLY-MORNING

Pair of vivid-yellow foam earplugs, to no avail. *2 pieces.*

Lengths 1 inch (2.54 cm)

11. TWO TAN OBJECTS
TWENTIETH-CENTURY

One a pepper mill and the other a salad bowl. Both somewhat the worse for wear. *2 pieces*

Height: 3 3/8 inches (8.16 cm)
Diameter: 6 inches (15 cm)

See illustration.

Drawings and Sculpture

12. ANONYMOUS
    BODY OF ALLIGATOR ON
    ASHTRAY BASE

Unsigned.
Ceramic, brown, yellow, blue and white.
Inscribed FLORIDA.

Height: 21 1/2 inches (54.5 cm)

See illustration.

13. FRAN LEBOWITZ
    A NUMBER OF DOODLES

Signed and dated '78.
Ballpoint pen under pressure.

5 × 3 inches
(12.7 × 7.6 cm)

14. FRIEND'S CHILD
"GOOD MORNING, MOM!"

Illegibly signed.
Crayon on coloring book.

*11 × 7 3/4 inches
(28 × 20 cm)*

See illustration.

"Good Morning, Mom!"

15. EDITOR
   DON'T WRITE TILL YOU GET WORK

Unsigned and rather dated.
Colored pencil on purloined office stationery.

8 1/2 × 5 1/2 inches
(21.5 × 14 cm)

See illustration.

16. RUGS

TWO RECENTLY LAUNDERED
COTTON TERRY BATHMATS
LATE NINETEEN-SIXTIES

The first rather mauve in color, the second an unusually common shade of blue; both nice. *2 pieces.*

Approx. 3 feet (.9 m) × 1 foot 8 inches (50.8 cm)

See illustration.

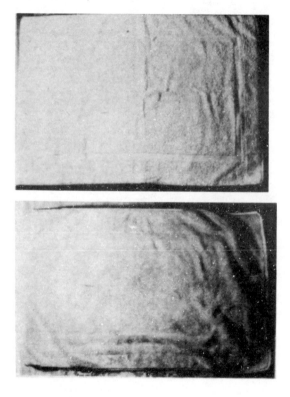

THE PEN OF MY AUNT IS ON THE OPERATING TABLE

A furnished apartment? No, I don't think so. I'm really not interested in a furnished apartment. No, really. Not at all. Not a furnished apartment. High tech? Yes, I know about high tech. Yes, I do. Really, I do. I know all about high tech.

I know about Sloan-Kettering too, but that doesn't mean that I feel like going up there and taking a look around.

No. Absolutely. No. Which building? Really? Oh, I love that building. That's a terrific building. I didn't know that you handled that building. You have an exclusive? Well. Aren't there any unfurnished apartments in that building? Oh. Yes, of course, the market. I know. I see. Yes, that's true, something else might come up there. Well, all right, but I'm really not interested in a furnished apartment. Not at all.

I can't believe this. I can't believe I'm going up there. A furnished apartment. I don't want a furnished apartment. A furnished apartment is out of the question. I hate furnished apartments. Although I can't imagine describing anything even remotely related to high tech as furnished. Equipped would be a better word, or maybe engineered. Every time I see one of those places I'm tempted to ask how many miles it gets to the gallon. Or where the boiler room is. Or the intensive care unit. The last time I was in a place like that I spent the better part of an hour skulking around looking for a brass plate inscribed with the name of the donor. High tech. I can't believe it.

Oh, hello. Yes, nice to see you again too. Sure, let's go right up.

Well, well, isn't this something. Oh, listen, I'm sorry but I don't seem to have a token with me. Do you think I could possibly borrow one from you? What? No turnstile? Yes, just an oversight, I'm sure. Some people just have no eye for detail. Then again, he may merely have been exercising his artistic restraint. He probably thought that the urinals in the living room were enough. A nice touch. Functional too, particularly for someone of his tastes—I mean taste. Well, now there's something I never would have thought of—a neon basketball hoop for a night light—it absolutely never would have occurred to me. It's quite an idea, though. Very thought-provoking. Visual humor. I've always loved visual humor. I wonder if I know anyone who knows Julius Erving? Probably not. Too bad, he might be interested in this. You know what they say about turnabout being fair play. Maybe at the next

*Philadelphia game he could shoot the ball into a night light.
He'd probably get a kick out of that. I know I certainly would.*

*Hmmmm, lookee there, will you. I mean, take a gander at
that. A genuine scrub sink with built-in instrument trays.*

No, no, I didn't notice that.

*A knee-controlled faucet too. Isn't that handy. Must be
just the thing for washing your hands when they're full. Yes,
it certainly does go beautifully with the chrome-plated hand
rails and hospital bathtub. All in all, I guess you'd have to
say that this is the bathroom that has everything. If you can't
get it here, you can't get it period. Scrub up, towel off and just
enough time for a little brain scan before bed. Nothing elaborate, just something to put your mind at ease and help you
sleep.*

The dining room? Of course, I'd love to see the dining
room.

*Look, let's be honest here. I'd love to see anything now.
Who knows how much time I have left? Anyway, maybe the
dining room will cheer me up. Maybe the dining room will
cheer me up? Who am I kidding? After that bathroom, open-
heart surgery would cheer me up. A weekend in Teheran with
the Ayatollah Khomeini would be a breath of fresh air. A visit
from the IRS would be like the month of May. Cheer me up?
I'll tell you what would cheer me up. It would cheer me up
if, in retaliation, the Ford Motor Company redecorated every
one of their plants in rose velvet love seats, fringed throw
pillows and teak cigarette tables. It would cheer me up if I
could sneak back in here tonight and pin a few doilies
around. It would cheer me up if tomorrow morning Congress
voted by an overwhelming majority to make the possession of
stainless-steel furniture a federal offense. It would cheer me*

up if only somehow I could arrange for my grandmother to get her hands on this place. Or Sister Parrish. Or my grand-mother and Sister Parrish.

Yes. Absolutely. A spectacular hallway.

A spectacular hallway? Listen, this would be a spectacular runway. I can see it now. A DC-10 coming in for a landing, refracted light glinting off the glass brick, right through here. Perfect. Masterful. The takeoff might be a problem, but what the hell, if it has to stay, it has to stay. There's simply no such thing as too much storage space.

Ah, the dining room. The dining room. Pretty impressive. No amphitheater, of course, but this place has probably been cut up. Undoubtedly the amphitheater is in the next apart-ment. Just my luck: no working amphitheater. Oh, well, this sure is a clean dining room. Nice long table too. Shiny, real shiny. And rugged. A nice mix. Must be interesting eating here. First a small but tasteful dish of number ten nails and then on to the Salk vaccine. I wonder what kind of wine you serve with the Salk vaccine. I wonder what you serve the wine in. You probably just inject it. I wonder where the syringe goes. On the left or on the right? What if it's a formal dinner and you're serving more than one wine? And what about the help? What if they're clumsy and a guest begins to bleed profusely? All over the rubber floor. Does blood come off rubber? I wonder if Pirelli makes actual dinner guests. Good, substantial, economically designed, pared-down dinner guests. Yes, rubber dinner guests, that's the ticket.

Big room. Very spacious. Maybe too spacious. Out of scale. If I owned this place I think I'd install two x-ray technicians a little off center at either end of the room. Fairly short x-ray technicians, about 5′5″, 5′6″, nothing taller. Bring the proportions down a little, make it more livable. And maybe, just to amuse the eye, a single black orderly set catty-corner right over there. Just one. On an angle. Yes.

The kitchen? Well, I'm not much of a cook myself, but sure, I've come this far, let's see the kitchen.

This is definitely the kitchen, all right, no mistaking it. I guess the mess hall must be back there. Lots of big stuff in here. Nothing namby-pamby about this kitchen. And talk about light, it's positively sunstruck. Couldn't possibly be depressed in this place. Not if you tried. No siree, no matter how many times you pulled K.P. you'd just have to smile. Nice counter, too. Pretty stools. What do they call this place, anyway—Joe's Co-op & Grill? Some kitchen. A lot of people could use a kitchen like this. Boys Town, for one. Nairobi. The International Ladies' Garment Workers' Union. AFTRA. Yes, indeed, a lot of people could use a kitchen like this. But somehow I'm afraid that I'm just not one of them. I mean, how would it look in that big glass-windowed refrigerator to see right on the shelf—yes, right over there, where the plasma should be—two grapefruits, an elderly piece of Swiss cheese and half a bottle of club soda? No, it just wouldn't look right.

The bedroom? Yes, the bedroom. No, I hadn't forgotten the bedroom.

Sleep? In here? Surely a joke. A cruel joke. Sleep, you say? For how long? Until when? What time is reveille around here, anyway? Five? Six?

Yes, I did. I did notice the bed. Seen one like it before? No, not really.

Not one that big, anyway. Certainly not that big. How could all the pieces fit in the box? Even the deluxe set.

No, I don't think I'll try it out, actually.

I've always been sort of squeamish. Silly, I guess, but I'm

*kind of afraid I'll cut myself. Nothing personal, mind you—
I mean I'm sure if you're careful, it's perfectly safe. Perfectly.*

Yes. Certainly. Go right ahead.

*In this place you probably need a dime. Maybe I can get
out of here before she's finished. I really don't know what to
say to her. Is she going to pressure me? Discuss financing? Do
you apply for a mortgage, or are you taken before a judge and
sentenced? She said something about low maintenance. I
wonder whether she meant that it was less than $750 a month
or that you could just hose the whole place down.*

*What if this sort of thing really catches on and people start
winning this stuff on game shows? Yes, that's right, Mrs.
Smith, twenty pounds of slotted-angle elements, and that's
not all—yes, Mrs. Smith, that's right, this beautiful three-
piece set of simple wire bicycle baskets too—all yours, Mrs.
Smith, and thank you for playing our game.*

*Oh no, here she comes. What will I say? I don't want to
insult her. After all, someday a* real *apartment might come
up in this building. I know. I'll tell her that I just can't afford
it, that it's out of my league, that it needs too much work. It's
a shame, though. I really do love the building. I wonder what
it would cost to take the cement walls down to the natural
mahogany paneling. No, out of the question. Just another
crazy dream.*

PLACES

PLACES

*P*erhaps one of the most notable features of contemporary life is the unprecedented expansion of the concept of freedom of thought. This has led to any number of unpleasant developments, but none more disconcerting than the fact that place, once that most fixed of entities, has now become a matter of personal opinion. This state of affairs has manifested itself in countless ways, and one can no longer take comfort and sustenance from knowing one's place, keeping one's place, taking one's place or finding one's place.

The list, of course, does not end here. I could and would go on and on, were there not a larger issue at stake. For the hazards set forth on this list, grave though they be, are relatively insignificant when measured against the knowledge that one's place of residence, traditionally a cold, hard fact, has now become subject to individual perception. Obviously, this is hardly a situation that can be allowed to continue. Therefore, at the risk of being labeled alarmist, I must state unequivocally that when one's own home, historically a representational art form, becomes vulnerable to what can only be called creeping conceptualism, it is high time that something be done.

Too late, you say? Time's run out? It's gone too far? I think not. There are still many of us left who, when asked where we live, reply with logic and conviction. New York, we say, or Boston. Philadelphia. Des Moines. We're a small group but a varied one, and I feel quite strongly that by hard work and perseverance we can vanquish forever those among us who, realizing instinctively that they could never win, decided instead to place.

The first step, of course, in any successful battle plan is to identify the enemy, and thus I have defined the following terms:

PEOPLE WHO THINK OF THEMSELVES AS INHABITANTS OF THE PLANET, OR EARTHMAN

Plainly given to gross generalization, Earthman is immediately recognizable by a relationship to green, leafy vegetables that can best be described as camaraderie. He eats and thinks low on the food chain and often believes in reincarnation—a theory that at least explains where he gets his money. His favorite book is something called *The Whole Earth Catalog,* from which he apparently orders his clothes, and he is so frequently to be seen gazing at the stars that one can only hope that he is thinking of moving.

PEOPLE WHO THINK OF THEMSELVES AS CITIZENS OF THE WORLD, OR INTERNATIONALMAN

Best typified by the big-time Italian fashion designer, Internationalman is at home wherever he goes. He knows all the best restaurants, all the best languages and is one of the few remaining people left alive to still carry cash—not to mention paintings. Although fun at parties, Internationalman has an effect that one is compelled to characterize as trivializing. What, after all, is London to a man who thinks of the whole Middle East as just another bad neighborhood and the coast of South Africa as simply the beach?

And how is it that with so much to do and see, Internationalman is still able to devote such huge amounts of time and attention to the driving up of co-op prices in the borough of Manhattan? An endeavor, I believe, which will eventually result in transforming the entire city of New York into a resort area comparable to Acapulco in the fifties. Here former native writers will be obliged to work in the kitchens of luxury hotels cutting grapefruits into fancy shapes for the pleasure of Internationalman—a customer who will not, by the way, probably be very much interested in meeting your virgin sister.

PEOPLE WHO LIVE TOO FAR DOWNTOWN, OR
LOFTMAN

People who live in lofts shouldn't throw stones, especially when they are in the enviable position of being able to sell them. Although SoHo has probably sprung to your mind, I am not, I assure you, that parochial, and can, due to unfortunate personal experience, report that such neighborhoods are now to be found in practically every minor American city. Usually occupying a renovated waterfront area, the quiche district, as I am wont to call it, has brought new and unwelcome meaning to the words "light industry."

You are advised that Loftman, appearances to the contrary, is really a fellow traveler of Earthman, and thus to be avoided assiduously.

PEOPLE WHO LOOK LIKE THEY LIVE AT THE SEATTLE AIRPORT, OR SALESMAN

Salesman, as he is commonly known, is a pretty harried-looking guy. Wandering as he does from gate to gate, it is no wonder that ofttimes he doubts his own sanity. Constantly he hears voices issuing instructions to what are openly referred to as "arriving Northwest Airlines passengers." It sounds very official; it even sounds real. Salesman, however, is nobody's fool and is well aware of the fact that there is no such thing as an arriving Northwest Airlines passenger—that when it comes to a Northwest Airlines passenger there is only a departing. In fact, at any given airport at any given time fully three quarters of the airport population consists entirely of departing Northwest Airlines passengers.

It is only to be expected, then, that people who spend so much time together would come to think of themselves as a community, with all that implies. Thus they have formed their own short-lived romantic attachments, developed their own cuisine based on the indigenous smoked almond and are enviably free of social unrest, having already been assigned classes by the airline.

Yet despite all this, Salesman is unhappy, for he knows that although he is headed straight for the top, he's just kidding himself to think he will ever really arrive.

LESSON ONE

*L*OS ANGELES, *laws AN juh lus,* or *laws ANG guh lus,* Calif., is a large citylike area surrounding the Beverly Hills Hotel. It is easily accessible to New York by phone or plane (although the converse is not true).

In 1956 the population of Los Angeles was 2,243,901. By 1970 it had risen to 2,811,801, 1,650,917 of whom are currently up for a series.

Early Spanish settlers called Los Angeles El Pueblo de Nuestra Señora la Reina de los Angeles, which means The Town of Our Lady, Queen of the Angels. The first part of the name was dropped when Los Angeles became a Mexican city in 1835. Today Los Angeles is often called collect.

The Land and Its Resources

LOCATION, SIZE AND SURFACE FEATURES

Los Angeles lies on the Pacific Coast approximately three thousand miles from midtown Manhattan. The terrain is varied and ranges from clay to grass to composition, depending upon the type of court you find most comfortable. Los Angeles is on the large side, covering over four hundred and fifty square miles, which makes it advisable to play close to the net.

Surface features are numerous, and include hills, palm trees, large billboards depicting former and future back-up singers, highly colored flowers, eye-tucks, parking attendants and an enormous sign spelling out the word "Hollywood," the purpose of which is to indicate that one has indeed gotten off the plane.

CURRENCY

The most popular form of currency in Los Angeles is the point. Points are what they give to writers instead of money. Curiously enough, it is impossible to use points to purchase either goods or services, a situation that makes imperative the possession of a round-trip airplane ticket.

CLIMATE

It is generally sunny in Los Angeles, thereby allowing the natives to read contracts by natural light. The mild weather is one of the main topics of conversation in Los Angeles, the other one being the lack thereof in New York.

Many tourists come to Los Angeles because of the climate, attracted no doubt by the pleasant glare and festive air colors.

CHIEF PRODUCTS

The chief products of Los Angeles are novelizations, salad, game-show hosts, points, muscle tone, mini-series and re-writes. They export all of these items with the twin exceptions of muscle tone and points, neither of which seem to travel well.

The People

Many of the people in Los Angeles appear so lifelike that a sharp eye is necessary in order to avoid conversation with those who may be too dead to offer points. Initiates will carefully study a prospective producer's gold neckchain and will not start talking until certain that it is moving rhythmically.

The inhabitants of Los Angeles are a warm people, and family ties are so strong that a florist may volunteer the information that his sister-in-law's stepmother was once married to Lee Major's great-uncle before one has had a chance to ask.

EVERYDAY LIFE AND CUSTOMS

Everyday life in Los Angeles is casual but highly stratified and can probably best be understood by realizing that the residents would be happiest with a telephone book that contained subscribers' first names, followed by an announcement that the party had four lines, sixteen extensions and a fiercely guarded unlisted number.

FOOD AND DRINK

A great many people in Los Angeles are on special diets that restrict their intake of synthetic foods. The reason for this appears to be a widely held belief that organically grown fruits and vegetables make the cocaine work faster.

One popular native dish is called gambei and is served exclusively in Mr. Chow's, an attractive little Chinese restaurant on North Camden Drive. The menu description of gambei reads as follows: "This mysterious dish is everybody's favorite. People insist it is seaweed because it tastes and looks just like seaweed. But in fact it is not. It's a secret." This mystery was recently solved by a visiting New York writer, who took one taste of her surprise and said, "Grass."

"Grass?" queried her dinner companion. "You mean marijuana?"

"No," the writer replied. "Grass—you know, lawns, grass. The secret is that every afternoon all of the gardeners in Beverly Hills pull up around the back, the cook takes delivery and minutes later the happy patrons are avidly consuming—at $3.50 per portion—crisply French-fried—their own backyards."

CULTURE

Los Angeles is a contemporary city, and as such unfettered by the confining standards of conventional art. Therefore the people of this modern-day Athens have been free to develop new and innovative forms all their own. Of these, the most interesting is the novelization, for this enables one, for perhaps the very first time, to truly appreciate the phrase, "One picture is worth a thousand words."

DRESS

The garb of Los Angeles is colorful, with lemon yellow, sky blue and lime green predominating, particularly in the attire of middle-aged men, most of whom look like Alan King. It is customary for these men to leave unbuttoned the first five buttons of their shirts in a rakish display of gray chest hair. Visitors are warned that calling the police to come in and button everyone up is a futile gesture; they will not respond.

Teenagers of both sexes wear T-shirts that disprove the theory that the young are no longer interested in reading, and facial expressions that disprove the T-shirts.

Middle-aged women favor for daytime wear much the same apparel as do teenage girls, but after six they like to pretty up and generally lean toward prom clothes.

THE LANGUAGE

Alphabet and pronunciation were both borrowed from the English, as was the custom of reading receipts from left to right. Word usage is somewhat exotic, however, and visitors would do well to study carefully the following table of words and phrases:

Formal: long pants

Concept: car chase

Assistant Director: the person who tells the cars which way to go. The phrase for this in New York is traffic cop.

Director: the person who tells the assistant director which way to tell the cars to go. The phrase for this in New York is traffic cop.

Creative Control: no points

Take a Meeting: this phrase is used in place of "have a meeting," and most likely derives from the fact that "take" is the verb that the natives are most comfortable with.

Sarcasm: what they have in New York instead of Jacuzzis.

TRANSPORTATION

There are two modes of transport in Los Angeles: car and ambulance. Visitors who wish to remain inconspicuous are advised to choose the latter.

ARCHITECTURE

The architecture of Los Angeles is basically the product of a Spanish heritage and a rich inner life. Public buildings, which are called gas stations *(gaz TAY shuns)* or restaurants *(res tur ONTS)*, are characterized by their lack of height and are generally no taller than your average William Morris agent, although they occasionally hold more people. Houses, which are called homes *(HOMZ)*, can be distinguished from public buildings by the number of Mercedes-Benzes parked outside. If there are over twelve, it is fairly safe to assume that they take American Express.

DIARY OF A NEW YORK APARTMENT HUNTER

*F*riday: Awakened at the crack of dawn by a messenger bearing this coming Sunday's *New York Times* Real Estate section. First six apartments gone already. Spent a good fifteen minutes dividing the number of *New York Times* editors into the probable number of people looking for two-bedroom apartments. Spent additional half-hour wondering how anyone who has a paper to get out every day could possibly have time to keep up eleven hundred friendships. Realized this theory not plausible and decided instead that the typesetters all live in co-ops with wood-burning fireplaces. Wondered briefly why listings always specify *wood-burning* fireplaces. Decided that considering the prices they're asking, it's probably just a warning device for those who might otherwise figure what the hell, and just burn money.

Called V.F. and inquired politely whether anyone in his

extremely desirable building had died during the night. Reply in the negative. I just don't get it. It's quite a large building and no one in it has died for months. In my tiny little building they're dropping like flies. Made a note to investigate the possibility that high ceilings and decorative moldings prolong life. Momentarily chilled by the thought that someone who lives in a worse building than mine is waiting for *me* to die. Cheered immeasurably by realization that a) nobody lives in a worse building than mine and b) particularly those who are waiting for me to die.

Saturday: Uptown to look at co-op in venerable midtown building. Met real estate broker in lobby. A Caucasian version of Tokyo Rose. She immediately launched into a description of all the *respectably* employed people who were waiting in line for this apartment. Showed me living room first. Large, airy, terrific view of well-known discount drugstore. Two bedrooms, sure enough. Kitchen, sort of. When I asked why the present occupant had seen fit to cut three five-foot-high arches out of the inside wall of the master bedroom, she muttered something about cross ventilation. When I pointed out that there were no windows on the opposite wall, she ostentatiously extracted a sheaf of papers from her briefcase and studied them closely. Presumably these contained the names of all the Supreme Court Justices who were waiting for this apartment. Nevertheless I pressed on and asked her what one might do with three five-foot-high arches in one's bedroom wall. She suggested stained glass. I suggested pews in the living room and services every Sunday. She showed me a room she referred to as the master bath. I asked her where the slaves bathed. She rustled her papers ominously and showed me the living room again. I looked disgruntled. She brightened and showed me something called a fun bathroom. It had been covered in fabric from floor to ceiling by someone who obviously was not afraid to mix patterns. I informed her unceremoniously that I never again wanted to be shown a fun bathroom. I don't want to have fun in the bathroom; I just want to bathe my slaves.

She showed me the living room again. Either she just couldn't get enough of that discount drugstore or she was trying to trick me into thinking there were three living rooms. Impudently I asked her where one ate, seeing as I had not been shown a dining room and the kitchen was approximately the size of a brandy snifter.

"Well," she said, "some people use the second bedroom as a dining room." I replied that I needed the second bedroom to write in. This was a mistake because it reminded her of all the ambassadors to the U.N. on her list of prospective tenants.

"Well," she said, "the master bedroom is rather large."

"Listen," I said, "I already eat on my bed. In a one-room, rent-controlled slum apartment, I'll eat on the bed. In an ornately priced, high-maintenance co-op, I want to eat at a table. Call me silly, call me foolish, but that's the kind of girl I am." She escorted me out of the apartment and left me standing in the lobby as she hurried off—anxious, no doubt, to call Cardinal Cooke and tell him okay, the apartment was his.

Sunday: Spent the entire day recovering from a telephone call with a real estate broker, who, in response to my having expressed displeasure at having been shown an apartment in which the closest thing to a closet had been the living room, said, "Well, Fran, what do you expect for $1,400 a month?" He hung up before I could tell him that actually, to tell you the truth, for $1,400 a month I expected the Winter Palace —furnished. Not to mention fully staffed.

Monday: Looked this morning at the top floor of a building which I have privately christened Uncle Tom's Brownstone. One end of the floor sloped sufficiently for me to be able to straighten up and ask why the refrigerator was in the living room. I was promptly put in my place by the owner, who looked me straight in the eye and said, "Because it doesn't fit in the kitchen."

"True," I conceded, taking a closer look, "that is a problem. I'll tell you what, though, and this may not have occurred to you, but that kitchen does fit in the refrigerator. Why don't you try it?"

I left before he could act on my suggestion and repaired to a phone booth. Mortality rate in V.F.'s building still amazingly low.

Called about apartment listed in today's paper. Was told fixture fee $100,000. Replied that unless Rembrandt had doodled on the walls, $100,000 wasn't a fixture fee; it was war reparations.

Tuesday: Let desperation get the best of me and went to see an apartment described as "interesting." "Interesting" generally means that it has a skylight, no elevator and they'll throw in the glassine envelopes for free. This one was even more interesting than usual because, the broker informed me, Jack Kerouac had once lived here. Someone's pulling your leg, I told him; Jack Kerouac's still living here.

Wednesday: Ran into a casual acquaintance on Seventh Avenue. Turns out he too is looking for a two-bedroom apartment. We compared notes.

"Did you see the one with the refrigerator in the living room?" he asked.

"Yes, indeed," I said.

"Well," he said, "today I looked at a dentist's office in the East Fifties."

"A dentist's office," I said. "Was the chair still there?"

"No," he replied, "but there was a sink in every room." It sounded like a deal for someone. I tried to think if I knew of any abortionists looking for a two-bedroom apartment. None sprang to mind.

Called real-estate broker and inquired as to price of newly advertised co-op. Amount in substantial six figures. "What about financing?" I asked.

"Financing?" She shuddered audibly. "This is an all-cash building."

I told her that to me an all-cash building is what you put on Boardwalk or Park Place. She suggested that I look farther uptown. I replied that if I looked any farther uptown I'd have to take karate lessons. She thought that sounded like a good idea.

Thursday: Was shown co-op apartment of recently deceased actor. By now so seasoned that I didn't bat an eye at the sink in the master bedroom. Assumed that either he was a dentist on the side or that it didn't fit in the bathroom. Second assumption proved correct. Couldn't understand why, though; you'd think that there not being a shower in there would have left plenty of room for a sink. Real-estate broker pointed out recent improvements: tangerine-colored kitchen appliances; bronze-mirrored fireplace; a fun living room. Told the broker that what with the asking price, the maintenance and the cost of unimproving, I couldn't afford to live there and still wear shoes on a regular basis.

Called V.F. again. First the good news: a woman in his building died. Then the bad news: she decided not to move.

FRAN LEBOWITZ'S TRAVEL HINTS

These hints are the result of exhaustive and painstaking research conducted during a recently completed fourteen-city promotional book tour. This does not mean that if your own travel plans do not include a fourteen-city promotional book tour you should disregard this information. Simply adjust the hints to fit your personal needs, allow for a certain amount of pilot error and you will benefit enormously.

1. It is imperative when flying coach that you restrain any tendency toward the vividly imaginative. For although it may momentarily appear to be the case, it is not at all likely that the cabin is entirely inhabited by crying babies smoking inexpensive domestic cigars.

2. When flying first class, you may frequently need to be reminded of this fact, for it all too often seems that the only discernible difference is that the babies have con-

PLACES   94

nections in Cuba. You will, however, be finally reas-
sured when the stewardess drops your drink and the
glass breaks.

3. Airplanes are invariably scheduled to depart at such
   times as 7:54, 9:21 or 11:37. This extreme specificity
   has the effect on the novice of instilling in him the
   twin beliefs that he will be *arriving* at 10:08, 1:43 or
   4:22, and that he should get to the airport on time.
   These beliefs are not only erroneous but actually un-
   healthy, and could easily be dispelled by an attempt on
   the part of the airlines toward greater realism. Understandably, they may be reluctant to make such a radi-
   cal change all at once. In an effort to make the
   transition easier I offer the following graduated alter-
   natives to "Flight 477 to Minneapolis will depart at
   8:03 P.M.":

   a. Flight 477 to Minneapolis will depart oh, let's say,
      eightish.
   b. Flight 477 to Minneapolis will depart around
      eight, eight-thirty.
   c. Flight 477 to Minneapolis will depart while it's still
      dark.
   d. Flight 477 to Minneapolis will depart before the
      paperback is out.

4. Stewardesses are not crazy about girls.

5. Neither are stewards.

6. You *can* change planes in Omaha, Nebraska.

7. You are advised to do so.

8. Whether or not you yourself indulge in the habit, always sit in the smoking section of an airplane. The coughing will break up the trip.

9. Whenever possible, fly with someone who is color-blind. Explaining to him the impact of rust, orange and yellow stripes against a background of aquamarine florals will fill the time you have left over from coughing.

10. When making bookstore appearances in areas heavily populated by artistic types, limit your signing of books "For Douglas and Michael" or "Joseph and Edward" or "Diane and Katy" to under ten copies. It will take you approximately that amount of time to be struck by the realization that you are losing sales. Announce pleasantly but firmly that it is common knowledge that homosexual liaisons are notoriously short-lived, and that eventually there will be a fight over your book. If this fails to have an immediate effect, remind them gently of the number of French whisks they've lost through the years.

11. It's not that it's three hours earlier in California; it's that the days are three hours longer.

12. Room-service menus that don't charge extra for cheese on hamburgers are trying to tell you something.

13. Fleeting romantic alliances in strange cities are acceptable, especially if you've already seen the movie. Just make sure that your companion has gotten the name of your publisher wrong.

14. Local television talk-show hosts are not interested in the information that the *Today* show uses more than one camera.

15. Twenty-four-hour room service generally refers to the length of time that it takes for the club sandwich to arrive. This is indeed disheartening, particularly when you've ordered scrambled eggs.

16. Never relinquish clothing to a hotel valet without first specifically telling him that you want it back.

17. Leaving a wake-up call for four P.M. is certain to result in a loss of respect from the front desk and over-familiarity on the part of bellboys and room-service waiters.

18. If you're going to America, bring your own food.

19. If while staying at a stupendously expensive hotel in Northern California you observe that one of your fellow guests has left his sneakers in front of his door, try to behave yourself.

20. Under no circumstances order from room service an item entitled "The Cheese Festival" unless you are prepared to have your dream of colorfully costumed girls of all nations rolling enormous wheels of Gruyère and Jarlsberg replaced by three Kraft slices and a lot of toothpicks dressed in red cellophane hats.

21. Calling a taxi in Texas is like calling a rabbi in Iraq.

22. Local television talk shows do not, in general, supply make-up artists. The exception to this is Los Angeles,

an unusually generous city in this regard, since they also provide this service for radio appearances.

23. Do not approach with anything even resembling assurance a restaurant that moves.

24. When a newspaper photographer suggests artistically interesting props, risk being impolite.

25. Absolutely, positively, and no matter what, wait until you get back to New York to have your hair cut.

26. Carry cash.

27. Stay inside.

28. Call collect.

29. Forget to write.

IDEAS

IDEAS

It was only to be expected that the era that gave us the word "lifestyle" would sooner or later come up with the concept of thoughtstyle. Thoughtstyle can probably best be defined by noting that in the phrase "lifestyle" we have the perfect example of the total being lesser than the sum of its parts, since those who use the word "lifestyle" are rarely in possession of either.

So too with thoughtstyle, and thus we find ourselves the inhabitants of a period during which ideas are not exactly flourishing—denizens, in fact, of a time when the most we can possibly hope to see are a couple of darn good notions. What is the difference, you may now be asking, between an idea and a notion? Well, the primary difference, of course, is that a notion you can sell but an idea you can't even give away. There are other differences, to be sure, and as can readily be seen by the following chart, I have taken care not to neglect them.

IDEAS	NOTIONS
MAKING CHANGE	ALGEBRA
ENGLISH	ESPERANTO
BLUEBERRY PIE	BLUEBERRY VINEGAR
POETRY	POETS
LITERATURE	THE NONFICTION NOVEL
CHOOSING	PICKING
BATHROOMS IN MUSEUMS	PAINTINGS IN BATHROOMS
LIGHT BULBS	LIGHT BEER
THOMAS JEFFERSON	JERRY BROWN
BREAKFAST	BRUNCH
DETROIT	SAUSALITO

While it may appear to the novice that this just about wraps it up, I am afraid that the novice is sadly mistaken. Ideas are, after all, a subject of some complexity. There are good ideas, bad ideas, big ideas, small ideas, old ideas and new ideas. There are ideas that we like and ideas that we don't. But the idea that I have seized upon is the idea that is not quite finished—the idea that starts strong but in the final analysis doesn't quite make it. Naturally, there is more than one such idea, and so I offer what can only be called:

A BUNCH OF HALF-BAKED IDEAS

TRIAL BY A JURY	OF YOUR PEERS
ADULT	EDUCATION
THE NOBLE	SAVAGE
HERO	WORSHIP
IMMACULATE	CONCEPTION
HIGH	TECH
POPULAR	CULTURE
FISCAL	RESPONSIBILITY
SALES	TAX
HUMAN	POTENTIAL
SUPER	MAN
MAY	DAY
BUTCHER	BLOCK
SEXUAL	POLITICS
METHOD	ACTING
MODERN	MEDICINE
LIVING WELL	IS THE BEST REVENGE

WHEN *SMOKE GET*
IN YOUR EYE ...
SHUT THEM

As a practicing member of several oppressed minority groups, I feel that I have on the whole conducted myself with the utmost decorum. I have, without exception, refrained from marching, chanting, appearing on *The David Susskind Show* or in any other way making anything that could even vaguely be construed as a fuss. I call attention to this exemplary behavior not merely to cast myself in a favorable light but also to emphasize the seriousness of the present situation. The present situation that I speak of is the present situation that makes it virtually impossible to smoke a cigarette in public without the risk of fine, imprisonment or having to argue with someone not of my class.

Should the last part of that statement disturb the more egalitarian among you, I hasten to add that I use the word "class" in its narrower sense to refer to that group more commonly thought of as "my kind of people." And while there are a great many requirements for inclusion in my kind of people, chief among them is an absolute hands-off policy when it comes to the subject of smoking.

Smoking is, if not my life, then at least my hobby. I love to smoke. Smoking is fun. Smoking is cool. Smoking is, as far as I am concerned, the entire point of being an adult. It makes growing up genuinely worthwhile. I am quite well aware of the hazards of smoking. Smoking is not a healthful pastime, it is true. Smoking is indeed no bracing dip in the ocean, no strenuous series of calisthenics, no two laps around the reservoir. On the other hand, smoking has to its advantage the fact that it is a quiet pursuit. Smoking is, in effect, a dignified sport. Not for the smoker the undue fanfare associated with downhill skiing, professional football or race-car driving. And yet, smoking is—as I have stated previously —hazardous. Very hazardous. Smoking, in fact, is downright dangerous. Most people who smoke will eventually contract a fatal disease and die. But they don't brag about it, do they? Most people who ski, play professional football or drive race cars, will not die—at least not in the act—and yet they are the ones with the glamorous images, the expensive equipment and the mythic proportions. Why this should be I cannot say, unless it is simply that the average American does not know a daredevil when he sees one. And it is the average American to whom I address this discourse because it is the average American who is responsible for the recent spate of no-smoking laws and antismoking sentiment. That it is the average American who must take the blame I have no doubt, for unquestionably the *above*-average American has better things to do.

I understand, of course, that many people find smoking

objectionable. That is their right. I would, I assure you, be the very last to criticize the annoyed. I myself find many—even most—things objectionable. Being offended is the natural consequence of leaving one's home. I do not like after-shave lotion, adults who roller-skate, children who speak French, or anyone who is unduly tan. I do not, however, go around enacting legislation and putting up signs. In private I avoid such people; in public they have the run of the place. I stay at home as much as possible, and so should they. When it is necessary, however, to go out of the house, they must be prepared, as am I, to deal with the unpleasant personal habits of others. That is what "public" means. If you can't stand the heat, get back in the kitchen.

As many of you may be unaware of the full extent of this private interference in the public sector, I offer the following report:

HOSPITALS

Hospitals are, when it comes to the restriction of smoking, perhaps the worst offenders of all. Not only because the innocent visitor must invariably walk miles to reach a smoking area, but also because a hospital is the singularly most illogical place in the world to ban smoking. A hospital is, after all, just the sort of unsavory and nerve-racking environment that makes smoking really pay off. Not to mention that in a hospital, the most frequent objection of the nonsmoker (that *your* smoke endangers *his* health) is rendered entirely meaningless by the fact that everyone there is already sick. Except the visitor—who is not allowed to smoke.

RESTAURANTS

By and large the sort of restaurant that has "no-smoking tables" is just the sort of restaurant that would most benefit from the dulling of its patrons' palates. At the time of this writing, New York City restaurants are still free of this divisive legislation. Perhaps those in power are aware that if the New Yorker was compelled to deal with just one more factor in deciding on a restaurant, there would be a mass return to home cooking. For there is, without question, at least in my particular circle, not a single person stalwart enough, after a forty-minute phone conversation, when everyone has finally and at long last agreed on Thai food, downtown, at 9:30, to then bear up under the pressures inherent in the very idea of smoking and no-smoking tables.

MINNESOTA

Due to something called the Minnesota Clean Air Act, it is illegal to smoke in the baggage-claim area of the Minneapolis Airport. This particular bit of news is surprising, since it has been my personal observation that even non-smokers tend to light up while waiting to see if their baggage has accompanied them to their final destination. As I imagine that this law has provoked a rather strong response, I was initially quite puzzled as to why Minnesota would risk alienating what few visitors it had been able to attract. This mystery was cleared up when, after having spent but a single day there, I realized that in Minnesota the Clean Air Act is a tourist attraction. It may not be the Beaubourg, but it's all their own. I found this to be an interesting, subtle concept, and have suggested to state officials that they might further exploit its commercial possibilities by offering for sale plain blue postcards emblazoned with the legend: Downtown Minneapolis.

AIRPLANES

Far be it from me to incite the general public by rashly suggesting that people who smoke are smarter than people who don't. But I should like to point out that I number among my acquaintances not a single nicotine buff who would entertain, for even the briefest moment, the notion that sitting six inches in front of a smoker is in any way healthier than sitting six inches behind him.

TAXICABS

Perhaps one of the most chilling features of New York life is hearing the meter click in a taxicab before one has noticed the sign stating: PLEASE DO NOT SMOKE DRIVER ALLERGIC. One can, of course, exercise the option of disembarking immediately should one not mind being out a whole dollar, or one can, more thriftily, occupy oneself instead by attempting to figure out just how it is that a man who cannot find his way from the Pierre Hotel to East Seventy-eighth Street has somehow managed to learn the English word for allergic.

THE LAST LAUGH

Coming from a family where literary tradition runs largely toward the picture postcard, it is not surprising that I have never really succeeded in explaining to my grandmother exactly what it is that I do. It is not that my grandmother is unintelligent; quite the contrary. It is simply that so firmly implanted are her roots in retail furniture that she cannot help but view all other occupations from this rather limited vantage point. Therefore, every time I see my grandmother I am fully prepared for the following exchange:

"So, how are you?"

"Fine, Grandma. How are you?"

"Fine. So how's business, good?"

"Very good, Grandma."

"You busy this time of year? Is this a good season for you?"

"Very good, Grandma."

"Good. It's good to be busy."

"Yes, Grandma."

Satisfied with my responses, my grandmother will then turn to my father and ask the very same questions, a dialogue a bit more firmly grounded in reality, since he has not deviated from the Lebowitz custom of fine upholstered furniture.

The lack of understanding between my grandmother and myself has long troubled me, and in honor of her recently celebrated ninety-fifth birthday I have prepared the following business history in order that she might have a clearer vision of my life and work.

My beginnings were humble, of course, but I am not ashamed of them. I started with a humor pushcart on Delancey Street—comic essays, forty cents apiece, four for a dollar. It was tough out there on the street; competition was cutthroat, but it was the best education in the world because on Delancey "mildly amusing" was not enough—you had to be *funny.* I worked ten-hour days, six days a week, and soon I had a nice little following. Not exactly a cult, maybe, but I was doing okay. It was a living. I was able to put aside some money, and things looked pretty good for a store of my own in the not too distant future. Oh sure, I had my troubles, who doesn't? The housewives browsing through every essay on the cart, trying to contain their glee in the hope that I'd come down a little in price. The kids snitching a couple of paragraphs when my back was turned. And Mike the cop with his hand out all the time looking for a free laugh. But I persevered, never losing sight of my objective, and after years of struggle I was ready to take the plunge.

I went down to Canal Street to look for a store, a store of my own. Not being one to do things halfway, I was thorough and finally found a good location. Lots of foot traffic, surgical supplies on one side, maternity clothes on the other—these were people who could use a good laugh. I worked like a dog getting ready for that opening. I put in a very reasonable ready-to-hear line, an amusing notions counter, a full stock of epigrams, aphorisms and the latest in wit and irony. At last I was ready; Fran's Humor Heaven: Home of the Devastating Double Entendre was open for business. It was tough going at first, but my overhead was low. I wrote all my own stock. And eventually I began to show a nice healthy gross and a net I could live with.

I don't know when it all began to go sour—who can tell about these things, I'm a humorist, not a fortuneteller—but business began to slip. First I took a bath with some barbed comments I was trying out, and then I got stuck with a lot of entertaining anecdotes. I hoped it was just an off season, but it didn't let up, and before I knew it I was in really big trouble. I tried everything, believe you me. I ran big sales— "Buy one epigram, get one free," "Twenty percent off all phrases." I even instituted a "Buy now, say later" plan. But nothing worked. I was at my wits' end; I owed everybody and was in hock up to my ears. So one day, pen in hand, I went to Morris "The Thesaurus" Pincus—a shy on East Houston who lent money to humorists in a jam. The interest rates were exorbitant but I signed my life away. What else could I do?

But it wasn't enough, and I was forced to take in a collaborator. At first he seemed to be working out. He specialized in parodies and they were moving pretty good, but before too long I began to get suspicious of him. I mean, I could barely put food on my table, and there he was, riding around in a Cadillac a block long. One night after dinner I went back to the store and went over the books with a fine-tooth comb. Just as I thought, there it was in black and white: the guy was a thief. He'd been stealing my lines all along. I confronted him with the evidence and what could he do? He promised to pay me back a few pages a week, but I knew that was one joker I'd never see again.

I kicked him out and worked even harder. Eighty-hour weeks, open every night until ten, but it was a losing battle. With the big humor chains moving in, what chance did an independent like me have? Then the day came when I knew all was lost. Sol's Discount Satire opened up right across the street. He wrote in bulk; I couldn't meet his prices. I, of course, was wittier, but nobody cared about quality anymore. Their attitude was "So it's a little broad, but at forty percent below list we'll forsake a little subtlety." I went in the back of the store and sat down, trying desperately to figure something out. There was a sharp rap at the door, and in walked Morris, a goon on either side, ready to collect. I told him I didn't have it. I begged for more time. I was pleading for my life. Morris stared at me coolly, a hard glint in his eye as he cleaned his nails with a lethal-looking fountain pen.

"Look, Fran," he said, "you're breaking my heart. Either you pay up by next Monday, or I'm gonna spread it around that you're mixing your metaphors."

With that he turned on his heel and walked out the door followed by the two gorillas. I was sweating bullets. If Morris spread that around, I'd never get another laugh as long as I lived. My head swam with crazy plans, and when I realized what I had to do, my heart thumped like a jackhammer.

Late that night I went back to the store. I let myself in through the side door and set to work. I poured a lot of gasoline around, took a last look, threw in a match and beat it the hell out of there. I was twenty blocks away when the full realization of what I'd done hit me. Overcome by remorse, I ran all the way back, but it was too late. The deed was done; I'd burned my comic essays for the insurance money.

The next day I met with the adjuster from That's Life, and thank God he bought the fire and paid me off. It was just enough to settle with Morris, and then I was broke again.

I started to free-lance for other stores, writing under a pseudonym, of course. My heart wasn't in it, but I needed the cash. I was grinding it out like hamburger meat, trying to build up some capital. The stuff was too facile, I knew that, but there was a market for it, so I made the best of it.

The years went by and I was just getting to the point where I could take it a little easy, when I was struck by an idea that was to change not only my own life but that of everyone in the entire humor business. The idea? Fast humor. After all, the pace had picked up a lot since my days on Delancey Street. The world was a different place; humor habits had changed. Everyone was in a hurry. Who had time anymore for a long comic essay, a slow build, a good long laugh? Everything was rush, rush, rush. Fast humor was an idea whose time had come.

Once again I started small, just a little place out on Queens Boulevard. I called it Rapid Repartee and used every modern design technique available. All chrome and glass, everything sleek and clean. Known in the business for my cunning and waggish ways, I couldn't resist a little joke and so used as my trademark a golden arch. No one got it. So I added another one, and got a great reaction. You really have to hit people over the head, don't you? Be that as it may, the place caught on like wildfire. I couldn't keep Quick Comebacks in stock, and the Big Crack was the hit of the century. I began to franchise, but refused to relinquish quality control. Business boomed and today I can tell you I'm sitting pretty. I've got it all: a penthouse on Park, a yacht the size of the *Queen Mary* and a Rolls you could live in. But still, every once in a while I get that old creative itch. When this happens I slip on an apron and cap, step behind one of my thousands of counters, smile pleasantly at the customer and say, "Good morning. Something nice in a Stinging Barb?" If I'm recognized, it's always good for a laugh, because, believe you me, in this business unless you have a sense of humor you're dead.

THE FRAN LEBOWITZ HIGH STRESS DIET AND EXERCISE PROGRAM

*E*ach year millions of people attempt to shed excess pounds by dint of strenuous diet and exercise. They nibble carrot sticks, avoid starches, give up drinking, run around reservoirs, lift weights, swing from trapezes and otherwise behave in a manner that suggests an unhappy penchant for undue fanfare. All of this is, of course, completely unnecessary, for it is entirely possible—indeed, easy—to lose weight and tone up without the slightest effort of will. One has merely to conduct one's life in such a way that pounds and inches will disappear as of their own volition.

Magic, you say? Fantasy? Pie in the sky? Longing of the

basest sort? Not at all, I assure you, not at all. No magic, no fantasy, no dreamy hopes of any kind. But a secret, ah yes, there is a secret. The secret of exploiting an element present in everyone's daily life, and using to its fullest advantage the almost inexhaustible resources available within.

That element? Stress. Yes, stress; plain, ordinary, every-day stress. The same type of stress that everyone has handy at any time of the day or night. Call it what you will: annoyance, work, pressure, art, love, it is stress nevertheless, and it is stress that will be your secret weapon as you embark on my foolproof program of physical fitness and bodily beauty.

DIET

The downfall of most diets is that they restrict your intake of food. This is, of course, galling, and inevitably leads to failure. The Fran Lebowitz High Stress Diet (T.F.L.H.S.D. for short) allows unlimited quantities of all foods. You may eat whatever you like. If you can choke it down, it's yours. The following is a partial list of allowed foods. Naturally, space limitations make it impossible to furnish a complete list. If you can eat something that is not on this list—good luck to you.

Allowed Foods

Meat	Candy	Rice
Fish	Nuts	Spaghetti
Fowl	Cereal	Sugar
Eggs	Cookies	Syrup
Cheese	Crackers	Pizza

Butter	Honey	Potato Chips
Cream	Ice Cream	Pretzels
Mayonnaise	Ketchup	Pie
Fruits	Jam	Wine
Vegetables	Macaroni	Liquor
Bread	Milk	Beer
Cake	Pancakes	Ale

As you can see, T.F.L.H.S.D. permits you a variety of foods unheard of on most diets. And, as I have stated previously, quantity is of no concern. I ask only that you coordinate your eating with specific physical activities. This program is detailed below.

EQUIPMENT

You can proceed with The Fran Lebowitz High Stress Exercise Program (T.F.L.H.S.E.P.) without the purchase of special equipment; it calls for only those accouterments that you undoubtedly possess already. A partial list follows:

Cigarettes
Matches or lighter
A career
One or more lawyers
One agent or manager
At least one, but preferably two, extremely complicated
    love affairs
A mailing address
Friends
Relatives
A landlord

Necessary equipment will, of course, vary from person to person, but T.F.L.H.S.E.P. is flexible and can adapt to almost any situation. This is clearly seen in the sample one-day menu and exercise program that follows. It must be remembered that it is absolutely mandatory that you follow exercise instructions while eating.

Sample Menu and Program

BREAKFAST

Large Orange Juice
6 Pancakes with Butter, Syrup and/or Jam
4 Slices Bacon and/or 4 Sausage Links
Coffee with Cream and Sugar
11 Cigarettes

a. Take first bite of pancake.
b. Call agent. Discover that in order to write screenplay you must move to Los Angeles for three months and enter into a collaboration with a local writer who has to his credit sixteen episodes of *The Partridge Family,* one unauthorized biography of Ed McMahon, and the novelization of the projected sequel to *Missouri Breaks.* (Excellent for firming jawline.)

MIDMORNING SNACK

2 Glazed Doughnuts
Coffee with Cream and Sugar
8 Cigarettes

a. Take first sip of coffee.
b. Open mail and find final disconnect notice from tele-
    phone company, threatening letter from spouse of new
    flame and a note from a friend informing you that you
    have been recently plagiarized on network television.
    (Tones up fist area.)

LUNCH

  2 Vodka and Tonics
  Chicken Kiev
  Pumpernickel Bread and Butter
  Green Salad
  White Wine
  A Selection or Selections from the Pastry Tray
  Coffee with Cream and Sugar
  15 Cigarettes

a. Arrange to lunch with lawyer.
b. Take first bite of Chicken Kiev.
c. Inquire of lawyer as to your exact chances in litigation
    against CBS. (Flattens tummy fast.)

DINNER

  3 Vodka and Tonics
  Spaghetti al Pesto
  Veal Piccata
  Zucchini
  Arugula Salad
  Cheese Cake

Coffee with Cream and Sugar
Brandy
22 Cigarettes

a. Arrange to dine with small group that includes three
    people with whom you are having clandestine love
    affairs, your younger sister from out of town, a business
    rival to whom you owe a great deal of money and two
    of the lawyers from CBS. It is always more fruitful to
    exercise with others. (Tightens up the muscles.)

As I have said, this is just a sample, and any combination
of foods and exercises will work equally well. Your daily
weight loss should average from between three to five
pounds, depending largely on whether you are smoking a
sufficient number of cigarettes. This is a common pitfall and
close attention should be paid, for inadequate smoking is
certain to result in a lessening of stress. For those of you who
simply cannot meet your quota, it is imperative that you
substitute other exercises, such as moving in downstairs
from an aspiring salsa band and/or being terribly frank with
your mother. If these methods fail, try eating while reading
the *New York Times* Real Estate section. Admittedly, this
is a drastic step and should not be taken before you have first
warmed up with at least six pages of Arts and Leisure and
one sexual encounter with a person vital to your career.

Occasionally I run across a dieter with an unusually stub-
born weight problem. If you fall into this category, I recommend as a final desperate measure that you take your meals
with a magazine editor who really and truly understands
your work and a hairdresser who wants to try something new
and interesting.

THE UNNATURAL ORDER

*N*ew Yorkers whose formative years were spent in more rural environments are frequently troubled by their inability to spot seasonal change. Deprived of such conventional signs as caterpillars, yellow leaves and the frost on the pumpkin, these bewildered citizens are quarterly confronted with the problem of ascertaining just exactly when it is what time of year. In an attempt to dispel this sort of confusion I offer the following guide:

AUTUMN

Autumn refers to the period beginning in late September and ending right before January. Its most salient visual characteristic is that white people all over town begin to lose their tans. New Yorkers, however, being somewhat reserved, it is not good form to try to rake them up and jump in them. Recent air-pollution control laws have also prohibited their burning, no matter how nostalgic one is for the homey scent of a roaring bonfire. Another marked feature of this season, and one not unrelated to the aforementioned, is that there *are* white people all over town, a fact worth noting in this context as it signals a mass return from the Hamptons (see Summer).

Nubbier, more textured fabrics start to make an appearance and shoes begin gradually to become more bootlike.

Politicians begin to spout brightly hued wild promises, but it is unwise to pick them, particularly early in the season, and on the whole one is far safer in sticking to the cultivated varieties.

WINTER

Winter begins where autumn leaves off, but has a lot more staying power than its quicksilver antecedent. As this season progresses one begins again to note fewer white people on the street (see Barbados) and more black people on television (see landlord's attitudes toward supplying heat; see landlords in person in Barbados).

Outdoor fashion shootings become sparse and are replaced by illegal aliens selling outsized pretzels and cold chestnuts.

Due to the dangers of the chill air, buses tend to band together in herds and Checker cabs pair off and retire to their garages for mutual warmth and companionship.

Although the frozen ground is hard and unyielding, often city contracts covering vital services come up for renewal (see Autumn, Spring and Summer) and mayoral press conferences are abundant.

Along about February, literary agents begin to turn green while talking on the telephone to their cinematic counterparts, and almost as one fly West to negotiate. Shortly after their return they will begin to lose their tans, but this is merely an example of the exception proving the rule and should not be taken by the novice as a sign of autumn. It is still winter, so try to regain your bearings by determining which out-of-season fruits are the most expensive.

SPRING

Rumored to be a season separating winter and summer, spring is, in New York, a rather mythical figure, and as such attracts a slightly rarefied crowd. Around April, art directors and aesthetic realists begin shedding their sweaters, and very constructed young men start to plan next autumn's colors. Property values on eastern Long Island rise sharply (see white people), while the level of reason and good will recedes from the banks.

Newsstands become more delicately tinged as magazine covers once again sport their seasonal pastel look and the word "relationship" is in the air, although fortunately not in the water.

Along about May, movie agents in Los Angeles begin to turn green while on the telephone to their literary counterparts and as one fly East to negotiate. Shortly after their arrival they will begin to lose their tans, but this will compel them to leave before even the rawest novice can think that it's autumn.

SUMMER

Although the most hard-nosed element maintains that summer is that time which is not winter, it technically describes the interval between spring and autumn, and most quickly manifests itself by a luxuriant growth in Con Edison bills.

The air becomes more visible, and a great many adults, stunned by the bountiful harvest of roving street gangs and sidewalk domino players, forget that they look terrible in shorts. Daylight-saving time blossoms once more and is welcomed heartily by insomniacs who now have less night to be up all of.

Wits thicken, urban flesh turns a vivid gray and the word "relationship" is in the water, but not, fortunately, in the city.

HOW TO BE A DIRECTORY AŞŞIŞTANCE OPERATOR: A MANUAL

INTRODUCTION

Uppermost in your mind should be the fact that as a Directory Assistance Operator your job is to serve the public. You must be helpful and courteous, of course, but serving the public is a grave responsibility and consists of a good deal more than might be immediately apparent. Give them the number, sure, but it must be remembered that the public is made up largely of people, and that people have needs far beyond mere telephone numbers. Modern life is such that the public has come to rely rather heavily on convenience, often forgetting the value and rewards of difficult, sustained labor. The human animal has an instinctive need for challenge, and you, as a Directory Assistance Operator, can be instrumental in reintroducing this factor to the lives of your charges. So serve the public, by all means, but do not make the mistake of thinking that serving the public compels you to indulge its every whim—for that, future Directory Assistance Operator, would be not only an error in perception but also a tacit admission of irresponsibility.

LESSON ONE: IS THAT A BUSINESS OR A RESIDENCE?

When a member of the public (henceforth to be referred to as the Caller) asks you for a number, do not even think about looking it up before you have inquired in a pleasant yet firm tone of voice, "Is that a business or a residence?" This procedure is never to be omitted, for doing so would display an improper and quite unforgivable presumptuousness on your part. Just because the Russian Tea Room doesn't sound like someone's name to *you* doesn't mean that it isn't. Americans *often* have strange names, a fact that has no doubt come to your attention no matter how short a time you may have been in our country.

LESSON TWO: DO YOU HAVE THE ADDRESS?

This lesson is of primary importance as it serves a twofold purpose. The first of these is to facilitate the process of finding the number in cases where there are many parties with the same name. Note that this is not the case in the aforementioned Russian Tea Room, who seems, poor man, to have no living relatives, at least not in Manhattan. The second and more important reason for asking this question is to make certain that the Caller is really interested in the *telephone number,* and is not imposing on your time and energy in a sneaky attempt to weasel out of you, the Directory Assistance Operator, an exact street address. You are, after all, employed by the New York Telephone Company, and are not under any circumstances to allow yourself to be badly used by some larcenous Caller trying to pull a fast one.

LESSON THREE: COULD YOU SPELL THAT, PLEASE?

The Caller will frequently respond to this query with an audible and unpleasant sigh, or in extreme cases an outright expletive. Ignore him absolutely. You are just doing your job, and anyway, what good reason could he possibly have for wanting to telephone someone whose name he won't or can't even spell?

LESSON FOUR: IS THAT "B" AS IN BOY?

In recent times this traditional, even classic, question has presented a rather touchy problem. Marches have been marched, laws have been passed, rights have been won. The sensitivity of the average member of the Third World has been heightened to the point where asking, no matter how respectfully, "Is that 'B' as in boy?" is apt to provoke an unseemly response. But since it is quite impossible, no matter how empathetic one may be, to logically inquire, "Is that 'B' as in man?," the modern Directory Assistance Operator is pretty much on her own here. Do, however, avoid "Is that 'B' as in black?" because you can never tell these days. And times being what they are, male Directory Assistance Operators assisting female callers are cautioned strongly against even thinking of risking, "Is that 'B' as in baby?"

LESSON FIVE: YOU CAN FIND THAT NUMBER LISTED IN YOUR DIRECTORY

This last procedure, coming as it does at the end of your long, often stressful association with the Caller, is the one most commonly neglected, particularly by the novice. Its importance should, however, not be underestimated, as it is well known that last impressions are lasting impressions. The Directory Assistance Operator is, as has been frequently illustrated in this manual, subjected to every sort of unattractive and condescending human behavior. "You can find that number listed in your directory" is your opportunity to establish once and for all that the Directory Assistance Operator is nobody's fool. "You can find that number listed in your directory" lets the Caller know, in no uncertain terms, that you have no intention of being pushed around by *anyone*, let alone anyone who, it seems, cannot even read the telephone book. So, for heaven's sake, never forget "You can find that number listed in your directory." It gets them every time.

ADDENDUM: HAVE A NICE DAY

The truly dedicated Directory Assistance Operator never fails to conclude the call with a sprightly rendition of "Have a nice day." "Have a nice day" is the perfect parting shot, not only because it shows once and for all which of you is the bigger person, but also because it has the eminently satisfying effect of causing the Caller to forget the number.

WAR STORIES

*D*espite my strenuous, not to say unparalleled, efforts to remain ill-informed, it has come to my attention that there has been, of late, some talk of war. Discussions concerning the drafting of women, the enrichment of the defense budget, and a certain unease on the part of older teenagers has led me to assume that what you people have in mind here is a regular war with soldiers, as opposed to a modern war with buttons.

Being classically inclined, I applaud this apparent return to the tried and true, yet cannot help but feel that contemporary life has taken its toll and we will thus be compelled to make certain allowances and institute practices that can only be called unorthodox. It is, therefore, in the national interests of a smooth transition and eventual victory that I offer the following:

SUPPOSE THEY GAVE A WAR AND YOU WEREN'T INVITED

The first step in having any successful war is getting people to fight it. You can have the biggest battlefields on your bloc, the best artillery money can buy and strategies galore, but without those all-important combat troops your war just won't get started. Numbers alone are not enough, however, and many a country has made the mistake of filling its armed forces with too many of the same type. A good mix is essential. Monotony is as dangerous on the battlefield as it is on the highway. The problem, then, is how to attract the sort of large and varied group that you are going to need.

The draft, of course, is traditional and always appropriate but it has, in recent years, fallen somewhat out of favor, becoming in the process not only old hat but downright ineffective. Clearly, extreme measures are called for, and in no way could they be better served than by the implementation of just a touch of psychological warfare. By combining the aforementioned situation with the indisputable fact that the grass is always greener on the other side of the fence, I suggest that instead of drafting, the powers that be consider inviting. Inviting ensures attendance by all but the most conscientious of objectors, who are impossible to get for really big things anyway. And although inviting might, at first glance, appear to be rather a grand gesture, the actual invitations can and should be simple and functional. Engraved invitations are showy, unduly formal and altogether lacking in urgency. The desired effect can probably best be achieved by the prudent use of the Mailgram. With the invitee's name and address in the upper left-hand corner a personal salutation is unnecessary.

We then proceed to the body of the Mailgram, which might, for example, read:

YOU ARE CORDIALLY INVITED TO
ATTEND THE ONLY PREDECLARATION

INDUCTION INTO THE ARMY FOR THE
UNITED STATES OF AMERICA'S
FORTHCOMING WAR. THE INDUCTION
WILL BEGIN PROMPTLY AT 8:00 A.M. AT
201 VARICK STREET, NEW YORK CITY ON
APRIL 15. WE REGRET THAT DUE TO
LIMITED SPACE ONLY ONE PERSON CAN
BE ADMITTED PER INVITATION.

R.S.V.P. TO OUR OFFICES ON OR BEFORE
MARCH 30. YOUR NAME ON OUR R.S.V.P.
LIST WILL EXPEDITE YOUR ADMISSION.

THIS INVITATION IS NOT TRANSFERABLE.

Only one person can be admitted per invitation? This
invitation is not transferable? Talk about impact. Imagine,
if you will, the days immediately following the receipt of this
missive. You are one of the lucky ones. There are others less
fortunate. First casual inquiries, then pointed requests,
finally desperate begging. On the eve of the induction the
truly insecure go out of town while the aggressively defen-
sive announce that they're exhausted and have decided to
just stay in and order Chinese food. Yes, people will be hurt.
Friendships will be dissolved. New, decidedly unappealing
alliances will be formed. It's too bad, but it can't be helped.
Blood, sweat and tears are no longer enough; nowadays you
need a door policy. All is fair in love and war.

THE CHILDREN'S CRUSADE

The most recent official statements on the subject indicate
that when it comes to war, the powers that be are partial

to eighteen- and nineteen-year-olds. The parents of these youths may understandably be disconcerted at having to send their children off to what is at best an unfamiliar environment. In an effort to assuage these fears, I suggest that they think of the army as simply another kind of summer camp, and keep in mind that their child may well be the one to return with that highest of honors: Best All-Around Soldier.

Camp Base

For Boys and Girls Ages 18–19
■ Our 102nd season as a friendly,
caring community ■ Complete
facilities ■ Hiking ■ Riflery ■
Overnight trips ■ Backpacking
■ Radar

EXTRA SPECIAL FORCES

Being in my absolute latest possible twenties, I am not myself of draftable age. That does not mean, though, that I am entirely without patriotism and the attendant desire to serve my country.

Desire is not, however (at least in this instance), synonymous with fanaticism, and I do feel that those of us who choose to go should receive certain privileges and considerations. The kinds of certain privileges and considerations I had in mind were these: either I go right from the start as a general or they establish, along guidelines set down by me, a Writers' Regiment.

Guidelines Set Down by Me

a. War is, undoubtedly, hell, but there is no earthly reason why it has to start so early in the morning. Writers, on the whole, find it difficult to work during the day; it is far too distracting. The writer is an artist, a creative person; he needs time to think, to read, to ruminate. Ruminating in particular is not compatible with reveille. Instead, next to each (double) bed in the Writers' Barracks (or suites, as they are sometimes called) should be a night table minimally equipped with an ashtray, a refreshing drink, a good reading lamp and a telephone. Promptly at 1:30 P.M. the phone may ring and a pleasant person with a soft voice may transmit the wake-up call.

b. In the army, discipline must, of course, be maintained and generally this is accomplished by a chain of command. In a chain of command you have what is known as the superior officer. The superior officer is fine for ordinary soldiers such as lighting designers and art directors, but the Writers' Regiment would, by definition, require instead something a bit different: the superior prose stylist. Having a superior prose stylist would, I am sure, be an acceptable, even welcome, policy, and will without question be adopted just as soon as the first writer meets one.

c. The members of the Writers' Regiment would, of course, like to join the rest of you in dangerous armed combat, but unfortunately the pen is mightier than the sword and we must serve where we are needed.

INTERNATIONAL ARRIVALS

Traditionally, former U.S. Air Force pilots have sought and attained employment with the commercial airlines. Today we can look forward to a reversal of this custom, as the U.S. Air Force becomes the recipient of commercially trained airline personnel:

"Hello, this is your captain, Skip Dietrich, speaking. It's nice to have you aboard. We're going to be entering a little enemy fire up ahead and you may experience some slight discomfort. The temperature in the metro Moscow area is twenty below zero and it's snowing. We're a little behind schedule on account of that last hit, so we should be arriving at around two-thirty Their Time. Those of you in the tourist cabin seated on the right-hand side of the plane might want to glance out the window and catch what's left of the wing before it goes entirely. That's about all for now, hope you have a pleasant flight and thank you for flying United States Air Force."

THE SHORT FORM

The poor are, on the whole, an unhappy lot. Ofttimes cold, invariably short of cash, frequently hungry, they unquestionably have grounds for complaint and few would dispute this. In general, the poor are deprived of most of the things that comprise that which is called "the good life" or "the American standard of living." This state of affairs has been duly noted by both the government and the governed, and much has been done in an attempt to alleviate the situation. Wherever a lack has been perceived a solution has been proposed. No money? Welfare. No apartment? Public housing. No breakfast? Food stamps. No tickee? No washee. No, that's another story. At any rate, you get my drift. The poor need help. The unpoor are willing —some, excessively so.

For those unpoor genuinely dedicated to good works it should come as no surprise that the dilemma of the poor extends far beyond that of the material. Lest you jump to conclusions, I should like to make immediately clear that I am not about to expound on the universal human need for love and affection. As far as I can tell, the poor get all the love and affection they can possibly handle. The concept of an unsuitable marriage obviously started somewhere.

No, I am not speaking here of emotional needs, but rather of those of a social nature. Needs of a social nature are perhaps the most complex and painful to discuss; yet they must be dealt with.

In order that you might gain a better understanding of this matter, I offer by way of illustration an imaginary dinner party (the very best kind) given by a member of the unpoor for his peers, you among them. You choose to accompany you a needy friend. He lacks the proper attire. You accommodate him from your own wardrobe. Your host provides ample food and drink. Your friend is momentarily happy. He feels unpoor, you feel generous, your host feels gracious, good will abounds. For just an instant, you toy with the notion that poverty could be completely eradicated by the simple act of including the poor in the dinner plans of the unpoor. Coffee is served. The talk becomes earnest. The conversation, as is its wont, turns to tax problems.

It is at this point, I assure you, that as far as the poor on your left is concerned, the party is over. Suddenly he feels poor again. Worse than poor—left out. He has no tax problems. He is, as they say, disenfranchised, dispossessed, an outcast, not in the mainstream. And under the present system he will remain in this degrading position for the life of his poverty. The double whammy. As long as he is poor he will be without tax problems, and as long as he is without tax problems he will, let us not forget, also be without tax benefits. And they call this a democracy. A democracy, when one man is in a fifty percent bracket and his dinner companion is in no bracket at all. It isn't enough that a man has no food, no clothing, no roof over his head. No, he also has no accountant, no investment lawyer, no deductions, no loopholes. And very likely no receipts.

This is, of course, unconscionable, and now that you have been apprised of the situation, it is unthinkable that it go on one minute longer—certainly not if we are to call our society an equitable one. Fortunately, there is a solution to this problem, startling in its simplicity, and one that should be implemented immediately.

Tax the poor. Heavily. No halfway measures. No crumbs from the rich man's table. I mean *tax*. Fifty percent bracket, property, capital gains, inheritance—the works.

Now, it has probably occurred to the careful (or even slovenly) reader that somehow this doesn't quite jibe. Something is amiss, you may say. The point you will be quick to raise is that the poor lack the means to be taxed. They cannot afford it. But I am ready for you, and will counter by saying that your inability to accept my solution is a matter of scale, of relativity. Let us examine each point separately.

FIFTY PERCENT

This is, naturally, the easiest to grasp, for it should be quite apparent to all that everyone has half, the poor included. If someone makes even as little as $1,000 a year, this still leaves him $500 for income taxes. Not a fortune, certainly, but still nothing to sneeze at.

PROPERTY

Your difficulty here is undoubtedly conceptual. That is, your conception of property very likely tends toward that fallow acreage, midtown real estate, principal residence sort of thing. It is true, of course, that these are all fine examples of property, but in a democracy who among us would deep down consider it really quite cricket to limit the definition of property to just the fine examples? After all, property merely means ownership; that which one owns is one's property. Therefore property taxes could—and should—easily be levied against the property of the poor. Equal freedom, equal responsibility. So no more free rides for hot plates, vinyl outerwear or electric space heaters.

CAPITAL GAINS

Now, this one is tricky but not insurmountable. And not surprisingly, the dictionary comes in handy. *Webster's Unabridged Second Edition.* The definition of "capital": *This accumulated stock of the product of former labor is termed capital.* And for "capital gains": *Profit resulting from the sale of capital investments, as stock, etc.* There, see? Another instance of relativity. Now. Uh. Yes. Um. Uh. Oh, all right, I admit it: it probably won't come up that often. But the poor would be well advised not to try selling off any leftover Spam Bake without reporting it.

INHERITANCE

Being creatures of habit, we ordinarily associate inheritance with death. Strictly speaking, we need not do so. Once again the dictionary proves most useful when it yields as a definition of "inherit": *To come into possession as an heir or successor.* Successor is, of course, they key word here. Thus, we can plainly see that while to some the word "inherit" may conjure up images of venerable country estates and

square-cut emeralds, to others—i.e., the poor—quite different visions spring to mind. A hand-me-down pair of Dacron
slacks is, of course, no square-cut emerald, but then again,
five hundred dollars is, as I believe I mentioned in point
number one, not a fortune, certainly.

AN ALPHABET OF NEW YEAR'S RESOLUTIONS FOR OTHERS

*A*s an answering-service operator, I will make every effort when answering a subscriber's telephone to avoid sighing in a manner which suggests that in order to answer said telephone I have been compelled to interrupt extremely complicated neurological surgery, which is, after all, my real profession.

*B*eing on the short side and no spring chicken to boot, I shall refrain in perpetuity from anything even roughly akin to leather jodhpurs.

*C*hocolate chip cookies have perhaps been recently over-valued. I will not aggravate the situation further by opening yet another cunningly named store selling these items at prices more appropriate to a semester's tuition at Harvard Law School.

*D*espite whatever touch of color and caprice they might indeed impart, I will never, never, *never* embellish my personal written correspondence with droll little crayoned drawings.

*E*ven though I am breathtakingly bilingual, I will not attempt ever again to curry favor with waiters by asking for the wine list in a studiously insinuating tone of French.

*F*our inches is not a little trim; my job as a hairdresser makes it imperative that I keep this in mind.

*G*ifted though I might be with a flair for international politics, I will renounce the practice of exhibiting this facility to my passengers.

*H*owever ardently I am implored, I pledge never to divulge whatever privileged information I have been able to acquire from my very close friend who stretches canvas for a famous artist.

*I*n light of the fact that I am a frequent, not to say permanent, fixture at even the most obscure of public events, I hereby vow to stop once and for all telling people that I never go out.

*J*ust because I own my own restaurant does not mean that I can include on the menu a dish entitled Veal Jeffrey.

K itchens are not suitable places in which to install wall-to-wall carpeting, no matter how industrial, how highly technical, how very dark gray. I realize this now.

L arge pillows, no matter how opulently covered or engagingly and generously scattered about, are not, alas, furniture. I will buy a sofa.

M ay lightning strike me dead on the spot should I ever again entertain the notion that anyone is interested in hearing what a fabulously warm and beautiful people I found the Brazilians to be when I went to Rio for Carnival last year.

N o hats.

O vereating in expensive restaurants and then writing about it with undue enthusiasm is not at all becoming. I will get a real job.

P olite conversation does not include within its peripheries questions concerning the whereabouts of that very sweet mulatto dancer he was with the last time you saw him.

Q uite soon I will absolutely stop using the word "brilliant" in reference to the accessories editors of European fashion magazines.

R aspberries, even out of season, are not a controlled substance. As a restaurant proprietor I have easy, legal access. I will be more generous.

Success is something I will dress for when I get there, and not until. Cross my heart and hope to die.

Ties, even really, really narrow ones, are just not enough. I will try to stop relying on them quite so heavily.

Unless specifically requested to do so, I will not discuss Japanese science-fiction movies from the artistic point of view.

Violet will be a good color for hair at just about the same time that brunette becomes a good color for flowers. I will not forget this.

When approached for advice on the subject of antique furniture, I will respond to all queries with reason and decorum so as not to ally myself with the sort of overbred collector who knows the value of everything and the price of nothing.

X is not a letter of the alphabet that lends itself easily, or even with great difficulty, to this type of thing. I promise not to even try.

Youth, at least in New York City, is hardly wasted on the young. They make more than sufficient use of it. I cannot afford to overlook this.

Zelda Fitzgerald, fascinating as she undoubtedly appears to have been, I promise to cease emulating immediately.

TO HAVE AND DO NOT

*N*ot too long ago a literary agent of my close acquaintance negotiated a book deal on behalf of a writer of very successful commercial fiction. The book in question has not yet been written. At all. Not one page. On the basis, however, of the reputation of the author and the expertise of the agent, the book-to-be was sold for the gratifying sum of one million dollars. The following week the same agent sold the same book *manqué* for the exact same figure to, as they say, the movies.

Soon thereafter I found myself seated at dinner beside the fellow who had purchased the movie rights to the book in question. I smiled at him politely. He smiled back. I broached the subject.

"I understand," said I, "that you have purchased A Writer of Very Successful Commercial Fiction's next book for one million dollars?"

"Yes," he said. "Why don't *you* write a movie for us?"

I explained that my schedule could not, at this time,

accommodate such a task, seeing as how I was up to my ears in oversleeping, unfounded rumors and superficial friendships. We were silent for a moment. We ate. We drank. I had an idea.

"You just bought A Writer of Very Successful Commercial Fiction's unwritten book for one million dollars, right?"

His reply was in the affirmative.

"Well," I said, "I'll tell you what. My next book is also unwritten. And my unwritten book is exactly the same as A Writer of Very Successful Commercial Fiction's unwritten book. I know I have an agent and I'm not supposed to discuss business but I am willing to sell you *my* unwritten book for precisely the same price that you paid for A Writer of Very Successful Commercial Fiction's unwritten book."

My dinner companion declined courteously and then offered me, for my unwritten book, a sum in six figures.

"Call my agent," I replied, and turned to my right.

The next morning I was awakened by a telephone call from said agent, informing me that she had just received and rejected the offer of a sum in six figures for the movie rights to my unwritten book.

"I think we can get more," she said. "I'll talk to you later."

I mulled this over and called her back. "Look," I said, "last year I earned four thousand dollars for the things that I wrote. This year I've been offered two sums in six figures for the things that I have not written. Obviously I've been going about this whole business in the wrong way. Not writing, it turns out, is not only fun but also, it would appear, enormously profitable. Call that movie fellow and tell him that I have several unwritten books—maybe as many as twenty." I lit another cigarette, coughed deeply and accepted reality. "Well, at least ten, anyway. We'll clean up."

We chatted a bit more and I hung up reluctantly, being well aware of how important talking on the telephone was to my newly lucrative career of not writing. I forged ahead, though, and am pleased to report that by careful application and absolute imposition of will, I spent the entire day not writing a single word.

That evening I attended an exhibit of the work of a well-known artist. I inquired as to the prices of the attractively displayed pictures, stalwartly registered only mild surprise and spent the remainder of the evening filled with an uneasy greed.

The next day, immediately upon awakening, I telephoned my agent and announced that I wanted to diversify—become more visual. Not writing was fine for the acquisition of a little capital but the real money was, it seemed to me, in not painting. No longer was I going to allow myself to be confined to one form. I was now not going to work in two mediums.

I spent the next few days in happy contemplation of my impending wealth. While it was true that no actual checks were rolling in, I was not born yesterday and know that these things take time. Inspired by my discovery, I began to look at things in an entirely new light. One weekend while driving through the countryside, I was struck by the thought that among the things that I cultivate, land is not one of them.

First thing Monday morning, I called my agent. "Listen," I said, "I know this is a little outside your field, but I would appreciate it if you would contact the Department of Agriculture and notify them that I am presently, and have been for quite some time, not growing any wheat. I know that the acreage in my apartment is small, but let's see what we can get. And while you're at it, why don't you try the Welfare Department? I don't have a job, either. That ought to be worth a few bucks."

She said she'd see what she could do and hung up, leaving me to fend for myself.

I didn't paint—a piece of cake. I grew no wheat—a snap. I remained unemployed—nothing to it. And as for not writing, well, when it comes to not writing, I'm the real thing, the genuine article, an old pro. Except, I must admit, when it comes to a deadline. A deadline is really out of my hands. There are others to consider, obligations to be met. In the case of a deadline I almost invariably falter, and as you can see, this time was no exception. This piece was due. I did it. But as the more observant among you may note, I exercised at least a modicum of restraint. This piece is too short —much too short. Forgive me, but I needed the money. If you're going to do something, do it halfway. Business is business.

ABOUT THE AUTHOR

FRAN LEBOWITZ lives in New York City, where she frequently makes jokes at the expense of others.